California Notary Handbook 2025

# California Notary Handbook 2025

## Your Ultimate Guide to Passing the California Notary Public Exam with Ease

Sophia L. Anderson

California Notary Handbook 2025

# DISCLAIMER

While every precaution has been taken in the preparation of this book, the publisher assumes no responsibility for errors or omissions, or for damages resulting from the use of the information contained herein.

California Notary Handbook 2025: Your Ultimate Guide to Passing the California Notary Public Exam with Ease

First edition.

# COPYRIGHT © SOPHIA L. ANDERSON 2025.
# ALL RIGHTS RESERVED

Before this document can be legally duplicated or reproduced in any manner, the publisher's consent must be gained. Therefore, the contents within this document can neither be stored electronically, transferred, nor kept in a database. Neither in part, nor in full can this document be copied, scanned, faxed, or retained without approval from the publisher or creator.

California Notary Handbook 2025

# TABLE OF CONTENTS

Disclaimer .................................................................................................. 2
Copyright © Sophia L. Anderson 2025. All Rights Reserved .................. 3
Table of Contents ...................................................................................... 4
Chapter 1 ................................................................................................... 7
   Introduction to the California Notary Public Role .............................. 7
      Overview of Notary Public Responsibilities ..................................... 7
      Importance of Notarial Acts in Legal Processes ............................... 9
      Qualifications and Eligibility Requirements .................................. 12
      The Commissioning Process in California .................................... 14
Chapter 2 ................................................................................................. 18
   Notary Public Laws and Regulations ................................................ 18
      Understanding California Notary Laws ......................................... 18
      Recent Legislative Updates Affecting Notaries ............................. 20
      Authorized Notarial Acts and Their Legal Implications ............... 23
      Prohibited Acts and Common Legal Pitfalls ................................. 25
Chapter 3 ................................................................................................. 29
   Notarial Acts and Procedures ............................................................ 29
      Acknowledgments .......................................................................... 29
      Jurats .............................................................................................. 31
      Oaths and Affirmations ................................................................. 34
      Copy Certifications ........................................................................ 36
      Handling Signature by Mark and Subscribing Witnesses ............. 39
Chapter 4 ................................................................................................. 43
   Notary Tools and Record-Keeping ................................................... 43
      Essential Notary Supplies .............................................................. 43
      Proper Use and Security of the Notary Seal .................................. 46
      Maintaining a Compliant Notary Journal ...................................... 49
      Record Retention Policies and Best Practices ............................... 52
Chapter 5 ................................................................................................. 56
   Identifying Signers and Preventing Fraud ........................................ 56

Acceptable Forms of Identification in California .................................... 56

Procedures for Verifying Signer Identity ................................................ 59

Recognizing and Addressing Signs of Coercion or Duress ..................... 63

Preventing Fraudulent Transactions and Impersonations ....................... 66

Chapter 6 ....................................................................................................... 70

Special Circumstances and Challenging Situations ..................................... 70

Notarizing for Non-English Speakers and Use of Translators ................ 70

Handling Documents for the Elderly or Disabled Signers ..................... 73

Remote Online Notarization: Current Status and Future Trends ............ 77

Dealing with Refusal of Notarial Services ............................................. 80

Chapter 7 ....................................................................................................... 84

Ethics and Professional Conduct ................................................................. 84

Ethical Principles Governing Notarial Practice ...................................... 84

Avoiding Conflicts of Interest ................................................................ 86

Advertising and the Use of Foreign Language Translations ................... 89

Legal Consequences of Misconduct and Negligence ............................. 92

Chapter 8 ....................................................................................................... 95

Preparing for the California Notary Public Exam ........................................ 95

Overview of the Exam Structure and Content ....................................... 95

Study Strategies and Time Management Tips ........................................ 97

Sample Multiple-Choice Questions with Explanations ........................ 100

Practice Exams to Assess Readiness .................................................... 104

Answer Key ....................................................................................... 113

Chapter 9 ..................................................................................................... 121

Post-Commissioning: Starting Your Notary Practice ................................ 121

Steps to Take After Receiving Your Commission ................................ 121

Bonding and Insurance Requirements .................................................. 123

Setting Fees and Managing Your Notary Business .............................. 126

Continuing Education and Staying Informed ....................................... 128

Chapter 10 ................................................................................................... 132

Resources and Appendices ......................................................................... 132

Glossary of Common Notarial Terms ................................................... 132

California Notary Handbook 2025
    Contact Information for California Notary Authorities ......................... 136

California Notary Handbook 2025

# CHAPTER 1
# INTRODUCTION TO THE CALIFORNIA NOTARY PUBLIC ROLE

## OVERVIEW OF NOTARY PUBLIC RESPONSIBILITIES

Notaries public hold a crucial position in upholding trust and authenticity within legal and administrative systems. Their primary responsibility revolves around serving as impartial witnesses to the signing of important documents, ensuring that these transactions are conducted with integrity and adherence to the law. To fully grasp the scope of their duties, it is essential to delve into the fundamental principles guiding notarial acts, the ethical and legal obligations involved, and the real-world implications of their role.

At the heart of a notary public's responsibilities lies the duty to verify the *identity* of individuals involved in a transaction. This task is not merely administrative but is vital to preventing fraud, forgery, and identity theft. Verification typically involves examining government-issued identification documents, such as passports or driver's licenses, to ensure they match the individual presenting them. In some jurisdictions, alternative forms of identification, such as credible witnesses, may be employed under specific circumstances. Regardless of the method used, the process must be conducted meticulously, as a lapse in diligence could lead to significant legal consequences for all parties involved.

Equally important is the requirement to ensure that signers are acting *willingly* and with full understanding of the document's contents. This responsibility underscores the notary's role in safeguarding against coercion or undue influence. For instance, if a notary observes signs of distress, hesitation, or confusion in a signer, it is their duty to pause the process and seek clarification. By doing so, they uphold the principle of informed consent, which is foundational to all notarial acts. This aspect of the role demonstrates the notary's commitment not only to the law but also to the ethical treatment of individuals.

Another key responsibility of notaries public is to administer oaths and affirmations when required. These solemn declarations are used in a variety of legal and administrative settings, such as affidavits or sworn statements. Administering an oath involves asking the individual to swear truthfulness under penalty of perjury, while an affirmation serves the same purpose but is offered as a non-religious alternative. The notary must ensure that the individual understands the gravity of the declaration and its legal implications. This task requires both clear communication and a firm grasp of the relevant legal standards.

The preparation and completion of notarial certificates form another essential component of a notary's duties. These certificates serve as official documentation of the notarial act, providing evidence that the procedure was conducted according to established legal protocols. Each certificate must include specific details, such as the date, location, type of notarial act performed, and the notary's official signature and seal. Accuracy in completing these certificates is paramount, as errors can render the entire transaction invalid. For example, omitting critical information like the signer's name or the type of identification used could result in disputes or legal challenges.

Maintaining a detailed and secure notarial journal is another cornerstone of notarial practice. The journal acts as a chronological record of all notarial acts performed, providing a transparent account of the notary's activities. Each entry should include essential information, such as the names of the signers, the type of document notarized, the method of identification used, and any fees charged. This record-keeping not only fulfills legal requirements in many jurisdictions but also serves as a protective measure for the notary in cases of disputes or allegations of misconduct. For instance, if a notarized document's validity is questioned, the journal entry can provide critical evidence to substantiate the notary's actions.

Confidentiality is another vital aspect of a notary's responsibilities. Notaries often handle sensitive information, including personal, financial, or legal details contained in the documents they notarize. It is imperative for notaries to respect the privacy of all parties involved and to safeguard this information against unauthorized disclosure. This obligation extends beyond the immediate act of notarization to include the proper handling and storage of records and materials. For example, a notary's journal should be kept in a secure location, accessible only to the notary or as required by law.

In addition to their standard duties, notaries may also encounter unique or challenging situations that require careful judgment and adherence to legal guidelines. For example, notarizing for individuals with disabilities or those who communicate in a language unfamiliar to the notary presents specific challenges. In such cases, the notary must ensure that all parties fully understand the document and the implications of their actions. This might involve using interpreters or alternative methods of communication, as permitted by law. Similarly, when dealing with transactions involving minors or other vulnerable individuals, the notary must exercise heightened vigilance to ensure compliance with legal and ethical standards.

The role of a notary public is also characterized by its neutrality and impartiality. Notaries must avoid any actions that could be perceived as favoritism or bias. This impartiality extends to avoiding conflicts of interest, such as notarizing documents for close family members or in situations where the notary stands to benefit from the transaction. By maintaining this neutrality, notaries reinforce public confidence in the integrity of the notarial process.

Education and ongoing professional development are integral to fulfilling the responsibilities of a notary public effectively. Many jurisdictions require notaries to complete training programs or pass examinations to ensure they have a thorough understanding of applicable laws and procedures. Continuing education is equally important, as it allows notaries to stay informed about legislative changes and emerging best practices. For instance, the growing adoption of remote online notarization (RON) in certain regions necessitates a deep understanding of the technology and legal frameworks involved. By staying updated, notaries can adapt to evolving demands and continue to serve their communities effectively.

The consequences of failing to adhere to notarial responsibilities can be severe, not only for the notary but also for the individuals and organizations relying on their services. Errors or misconduct, whether intentional or accidental, can lead to financial losses, legal disputes, and damage to the notary's professional reputation. In extreme cases, notaries may face civil or criminal penalties, including fines, suspension, or revocation of their commission. These potential repercussions underscore the importance of diligence, accuracy, and ethical conduct in all aspects of notarial practice.

To illustrate the impact of a notary's responsibilities, consider the example of a real estate transaction. A buyer and seller agree on the sale of a property, and the notary's role is to witness the signing of the deed and verify the identities of the parties involved. If the notary fails to properly authenticate the identification documents or overlooks signs of forgery, the transaction could be contested, leading to costly legal battles. Conversely, a notary who performs their duties with precision and integrity ensures a smooth process, providing peace of mind to all parties and contributing to the reliability of the legal system.

Notaries public also play a significant role in fostering international commerce and legal cooperation. Many cross-border transactions require notarized documents to ensure their validity and acceptance in foreign jurisdictions. In such cases, the notary's responsibilities extend to understanding and complying with international requirements, such as obtaining an apostille under the Hague Apostille Convention. This global dimension of notarial practice highlights the profession's importance in facilitating trust and collaboration across borders.

## IMPORTANCE OF NOTARIAL ACTS IN LEGAL PROCESSES

Notarial acts play a *pivotal role* in ensuring the integrity, authenticity, and reliability of legal processes. By performing duties that verify the identities of individuals and the voluntary nature of their actions, notaries act as trusted intermediaries between private citizens and the legal system. In California, the responsibilities of a notary public are especially significant, as the state's complex legal framework heavily relies on notarization to uphold public trust in documents and transactions. Whether it involves preventing fraud, establishing authenticity, or providing an official layer of validation to legal transactions, notarial acts ensure that critical processes flow smoothly and remain enforceable.

The foundation of a notarial act lies in its ability to authenticate and formalize documents. When individuals engage in legal processes such as signing contracts, transferring property, or executing wills, the integrity of these transactions depends on the certainty that they were carried out *willingly* and by the *correct parties*. Without this assurance, legal disputes would become commonplace, and the enforcement of agreements would face constant challenges. For example, consider a case where an individual signs over the deed to a property without proper notarization. If the deed were later disputed in court, the absence of notarization could cast doubt on the signer's intent or identity, leaving the transaction open to being declared invalid. A notary's role ensures that such ambiguities are eliminated from the outset.

One of the key ways notaries achieve this is by verifying the identity of all parties involved in a transaction. In California, strict guidelines dictate the forms of identification a notary can accept, such as government-issued IDs or passports. This safeguard ensures that the person signing a document is exactly who they claim to be. Imagine a scenario where a fraudulent individual attempts to impersonate another to sell property or access sensitive records. Without a notary to rigorously confirm their identity, the potential for fraud would be immense. The notary serves as a frontline defense, scrutinizing identification and cross-referencing details to prevent such occurrences.

Equally important is the notary's duty to confirm the *voluntary nature* of a signer's actions. In California, notaries are trained to observe signs of coercion, duress, or manipulation during the signing process. If a notary suspects that an individual is being pressured or does not fully understand the implications of what they are signing, they are obligated to halt the process. This is particularly vital in cases involving vulnerable populations, such as the elderly or individuals with limited language proficiency. For example, an older adult preparing to transfer their estate may face pressure from a relative. A diligent notary, upon sensing hesitation or discomfort, would take the necessary steps to pause the notarization and address the concern, ensuring the act remains ethical and legally sound.

Notarial acts also provide an official record of important transactions. By maintaining detailed journals, California notaries create a reliable trail of evidence that can be referenced in disputes or legal inquiries. These journals include critical information such as the date and type of transaction, the identity of the signer, and the notary's own observations during the process. This record-keeping adds a layer of accountability, making it possible to verify the circumstances under which a document was signed. For instance, in the event of a contested loan agreement, the notary's journal could serve as vital evidence confirming that the signer appeared voluntarily and presented valid identification. Without such records, parties might struggle to resolve disputes, leading to unnecessary delays and complications.

The significance of notarial acts extends beyond the individual transactions they facilitate. On a broader scale, notarization upholds the *credibility of the legal system* itself. Legal systems rely on the assumption that signed documents are authentic and represent the true intentions of the parties involved. By enforcing this standard through notarization, notaries contribute to the public's confidence in contracts, deeds, affidavits, and other legal instruments. For example, a company entering into a multimillion-dollar merger depends on the notarized signatures of its executives to ensure that the agreement is legally binding. Any doubt regarding the authenticity of these signatures could derail the merger, causing financial losses and reputational harm. The notary's seal eliminates such uncertainties, allowing complex transactions to proceed with confidence.

Beyond their role in authentication, notarial acts are vital for facilitating access to justice and legal protections. Many legal processes, such as filing affidavits, applying for immigration benefits, or securing powers of attorney, require notarized documentation. These acts make it possible for individuals to assert their rights and navigate legal systems effectively. For instance, an immigrant seeking to adjust their legal status in the United States may need to submit notarized forms affirming certain facts about their residence or employment. Without notarization, these forms would lack the weight of legal credibility, potentially delaying or jeopardizing the outcome. In this sense, notaries serve as enablers of justice, ensuring that individuals can participate fully in the legal processes that shape their lives.

Notaries also play a critical role in protecting the interests of businesses and organizations. In California's robust economy, where transactions often involve high stakes, notarization acts as a safeguard against financial and reputational risks. A commercial lease agreement, for example, often requires notarization to ensure that both parties are legally bound by its terms. If a dispute arises regarding the validity of the lease, the notarization provides clear evidence that the agreement was executed properly. Similarly, businesses engaging in cross-border trade may rely on notarized documents to comply with international regulations and establish trust with foreign partners. These acts not only protect individual parties but also contribute to the stability and reliability of the broader economic landscape.

The importance of notarial acts is further underscored by their role in preventing fraudulent activities. In a digital age where forgery and identity theft are increasingly sophisticated, the presence of a notary serves as a crucial line of defense. By carefully examining signatures, verifying identities, and adhering to standardized procedures, notaries make it exponentially more difficult for fraudulent actors to succeed. For example, a scammer attempting to alter a will for financial gain would find it nearly impossible to bypass the scrutiny of a trained notary. The notarial act, therefore, acts as a deterrent, dissuading individuals from attempting dishonest or unethical behavior in the first place.

Additionally, the legal enforceability of documents often hinges on the presence of a notarized acknowledgment or jurat. California courts frequently require notarized affidavits, contracts, and declarations to proceed with cases. The absence of notarization can render these documents inadmissible, delaying proceedings and complicating legal resolutions. Consider a case where a family disputes the terms of a prenuptial agreement. If the agreement lacks proper notarization, the court may question its validity, leading to further litigation. A notarized document, by contrast, stands as a definitive and enforceable record, expediting the resolution of disputes and ensuring that justice is served efficiently.

Notarial acts also hold cultural and symbolic significance. The notary's seal, often viewed as a mark of authenticity, carries a weight of authority and professionalism. It reassures signers and recipients alike that a document has been executed with due care and in compliance with the law. This perception enhances trust not only in individual transactions but also in the notarial profession as a whole. In California, where the notarial community serves a diverse population with varying legal needs, the consistency and reliability of notarial acts foster a sense of security and fairness across different cultural and economic contexts.

The value of notarial acts can also be observed in their contribution to international legal processes. In cross-border transactions or immigration cases, notarized documents often serve as the foundation for legal recognition in foreign jurisdictions. For example, an individual applying for a visa may need to present notarized copies of their birth certificate or marriage license. These documents, authenticated by a California notary, provide the assurance that foreign authorities require to proceed with the application. In such instances, the notary acts as a bridge between legal systems, facilitating cooperation and mutual recognition across borders.

At every level, notarial acts are indispensable to the smooth functioning of legal and societal processes. From safeguarding individual rights to supporting global commerce, the work of notaries ensures that transactions are conducted with integrity and trust. By performing their duties with diligence and professionalism, notaries contribute not only to the resolution of individual legal matters but also to the broader principles of fairness and justice that underpin a stable society.

## QUALIFICATIONS AND ELIGIBILITY REQUIREMENTS

Becoming a notary public in California is both an opportunity and a responsibility. Notaries play a vital role in ensuring the integrity and reliability of countless transactions, acting as impartial witnesses and custodians of trust. The qualifications and eligibility requirements for becoming a notary in California reflect the importance of this role, ensuring that those who serve as notaries meet the highest standards of character, knowledge, and reliability. Each of these requirements is designed to ensure that notaries can perform their duties with competence and professionalism, while also protecting the public from potential fraud or misconduct.

To qualify as a notary public in California, an applicant must first meet specific basic eligibility criteria. One of the most fundamental requirements is that the applicant must be at least *18 years of age*. This age threshold ensures that individuals appointed as notaries possess the maturity necessary to handle sensitive and legally significant responsibilities. A notary must often evaluate the voluntary nature of a signer's actions, detect signs of fraud, and maintain meticulous records, all of which require a level of judgment typically associated with adulthood. For instance, a notary might encounter a situation where a signer appears unsure about the document they are about to sign. In such cases, the notary must confidently pause the transaction and address the concerns, which is why the maturity associated with adulthood is critical.

Another key requirement is *legal residency in the state of California*. Only individuals who reside within the state are eligible to apply for a California notary public commission. This requirement ensures that the notary is familiar with California's laws, cultural context, and legal practices, all of which are essential for effective service. A notary who lives and works in California is more likely to understand the specific needs of the state's diverse communities, whether assisting a business with notarizing a loan agreement or helping an immigrant family with essential legal documents.

California also requires that all applicants possess the ability to read, write, and understand *English*. This linguistic proficiency is crucial because notaries are responsible for reviewing and completing official forms, understanding complex legal terminology, and ensuring that the documents they notarize are accurate. Imagine a scenario in which a notary is unable to understand a legal term or instruction; the potential for errors or omissions would be significant, potentially jeopardizing the legality of the transaction. This requirement, therefore, ensures that all notaries are equipped to engage fully with the documents and legal frameworks they encounter.

The *absence of disqualifying criminal convictions* is another critical eligibility criterion. Applicants must disclose their criminal history and undergo a thorough background check conducted by the California Department of Justice and the Federal Bureau of Investigation (FBI). Certain convictions, particularly those involving dishonesty, fraud, or theft, may disqualify an individual from serving as a notary. This safeguard protects the public by ensuring that only individuals with a proven track record of trustworthiness and integrity are entrusted with the role of a notary public. For example, a person with a history of fraudulent activities might exploit the notarial process for personal gain, undermining the integrity of the entire profession. By requiring a clean criminal record, California ensures that its notaries are worthy of the public's trust.

Applicants must also complete a state-approved *notary public education course*. This requirement ensures that aspiring notaries have a thorough understanding of California's notary laws, practices, and ethical standards. The course typically spans six hours and covers a wide range of topics, including the proper administration of acknowledgments, jurats, and oaths; the correct use of a notary seal and journal; and the steps to take when dealing with unusual or challenging situations. For instance, the course may address how to handle a signer who presents an expired identification card or how to recognize signs of coercion. Completing this education requirement equips applicants with the knowledge they need to handle their responsibilities with confidence and competence.

Upon completing the education course, applicants must pass a *written exam* administered by the California Secretary of State's office. This exam tests the applicant's understanding of the laws and practices covered in the education course, ensuring that they are well-prepared to perform their duties as notaries. The exam consists of multiple-choice questions and requires a minimum passing score to demonstrate proficiency. For example, a question on the exam might ask an applicant to identify the correct procedure for notarizing a document for a signer who does not speak English. By passing the exam, applicants demonstrate that they have mastered the knowledge necessary to navigate real-world scenarios with professionalism.

Once the education and exam requirements are satisfied, applicants must submit a *notary public application* to the California Secretary of State, along with the appropriate filing fee. This application includes a detailed personal history, as well as information about the applicant's education, employment, and any prior notary commissions. The application process also involves the submission of fingerprints for the aforementioned background check. These steps are designed to ensure that all applicants are thoroughly vetted before they are entrusted with the responsibilities of a notary public.

An essential part of the qualification process is obtaining a *surety bond*. California law requires all notaries to secure a $15,000 bond, which serves as a financial guarantee to protect the public from losses resulting from a notary's errors or misconduct. The bond does not protect the notary personally; rather, it provides a remedy for individuals who may be harmed by the notary's actions. For example, if a notary improperly notarizes a document that leads to financial harm, the injured party may file a claim against the bond to recover their losses. The bond requirement underscores the seriousness of the notary's role and the potential consequences of negligence or wrongdoing.

After completing these steps, the final requirement is to take an *oath of office*. This oath is administered by the county clerk's office in the county where the notary will serve. By taking the oath, the notary formally pledges to perform their duties with integrity, impartiality, and adherence to the law. This ceremonial step marks the culmination of the qualification process and signifies the notary's official entry into their role as a public servant.

Once commissioned, notaries must remain vigilant about maintaining their eligibility. This includes renewing their commission every four years, completing continuing education courses, and adhering to all applicable laws and regulations. For instance, if a notary moves to a different county within California, they must update their address with the Secretary of State to ensure that their commission remains valid. Similarly, if a notary's seal is lost or stolen, they must report it immediately to prevent potential misuse.

These qualifications and eligibility requirements reflect the high standards that California sets for its notaries public. By ensuring that applicants possess the necessary skills, knowledge, and integrity, the state protects the public from fraud and misconduct while upholding the credibility of the notarial profession. Every step of the process, from the education course to the oath of office, is designed to prepare notaries for the challenges they may face and to reinforce the public's trust in their vital role.

## THE COMMISSIONING PROCESS IN CALIFORNIA

The commissioning process in California is an essential step in becoming a legally recognized Notary Public, and it involves several key stages that ensure individuals are qualified and prepared to perform notarizations with integrity and accuracy. Understanding this process is crucial for anyone interested in becoming a Notary in California, as it provides the foundation for their responsibilities and obligations. Whether you're considering this path or have already embarked on it, knowing the detailed steps of the commissioning process is vital to performing your duties effectively and in accordance with California law.

The first and perhaps most obvious step in the commissioning process is to meet the basic eligibility requirements set forth by the California Secretary of State. These requirements are in place to ensure that all applicants are of sound character and can carry out the duties of a Notary Public responsibly. The applicant must be at least 18 years old and a legal resident of California. If you're not a U.S. citizen, you must still be a legal resident, meaning you are authorized to live and work in the United States. It's important to understand that California law is strict when it comes to the eligibility of potential notaries, so meeting these basic criteria is the first hurdle that applicants must clear.

After confirming eligibility, the next critical step is completing the application. The application process is fairly straightforward, but it requires careful attention to detail to ensure accuracy. The form is available online through the California Secretary of State's website, and it can be filled out electronically or printed for manual submission. As you complete this form, you will need to provide personal details, such as your name, address, and contact information. It's essential that the information is correct and matches any official documents, as discrepancies could delay the approval process. You will also be asked if you have ever been convicted of a felony, as this may disqualify you from obtaining a Notary commission.

Once your application is complete, the next step is to undergo a background check. California requires all applicants to undergo a criminal background check through Live Scan fingerprinting. This is a critical part of the process, as it helps to ensure that only individuals with a clean criminal record are appointed as Notaries Public. The fingerprinting process is done through authorized locations, and the results are sent directly to the California Secretary of State's office. While it may seem like a straightforward task, it's important to understand that this process can take several weeks to complete, so patience is necessary.

After passing the background check, applicants are required to take and pass a written exam. The exam is designed to test your knowledge of California notarial laws and practices, ensuring that you understand the responsibilities you will undertake as a Notary Public. The test is not to be taken lightly, as it covers various aspects of the law, including the identification of signers, proper document handling, and understanding when and how to refuse a notarization. The exam typically consists of 30 multiple-choice questions, and you must score at least 70% to pass. Preparing for the exam involves studying the materials provided by the California Secretary of State and familiarizing yourself with the relevant laws and regulations. Many applicants find it helpful to take preparatory courses to boost their knowledge and ensure they are fully prepared for the test.

Once you have successfully completed the written exam, you are ready to submit your application along with proof of the completed fingerprinting and exam results to the Secretary of State's office. At this point, it's important to understand that there are fees associated with the commissioning process. These fees include the application fee, the fingerprinting fee, and any other costs related to the preparation and submission of your materials. The exact amount can vary, but it's essential to budget accordingly and ensure that all fees are paid on time to avoid delays in the process.

If your application is approved, the next step is to take an oath of office. The oath is a formal declaration in which you promise to uphold the duties of a Notary Public and perform your duties honestly and ethically. This is a serious commitment, and it's a step that should not be taken lightly. The oath can be administered by a current Notary Public, a judge, or another authorized official. After taking the oath, you are officially a Notary Public, and your commission is valid for a period of four years.

Now that you are a commissioned Notary Public in California, it's important to understand your responsibilities and the practical steps involved in carrying out your duties. One of the first things you will need to do is obtain a Notary seal. This seal is used to authenticate the documents you notarize and serves as a symbol of your authority as a Notary Public. In California, the Notary seal must meet specific requirements, such as including your name, the words "Notary Public," and the county where your oath of office was taken. It is your responsibility to ensure that your seal is always used properly, and it must be kept secure at all times to prevent misuse.

In addition to the Notary seal, you will also need to keep a journal of all notarizations you perform. This journal is a critical record of your activities and is required by California law. The journal should include details such as the date and time of the notarization, the type of document being notarized, the names of the signers, and a description of the identification presented by the signers. Keeping an accurate and up-to-date journal is not only a legal requirement but also a safeguard in the event that your notarizations are ever questioned or challenged.

Another important aspect of the commissioning process is the ongoing responsibility to stay informed about any changes to notarial laws and regulations. As a Notary Public, you must adhere to all current state laws, and failure to do so can result in penalties, including the loss of your commission. It's your responsibility to regularly review the laws and ensure that you are up to date on any changes that may affect your duties. This can be done through resources provided by the California Secretary of State or by joining professional organizations that offer training and updates on notarial practices.

Throughout your time as a Notary Public, you must also be aware of the situations in which you may refuse to perform a notarization. California law allows Notaries to refuse services in certain circumstances, such as when a signer is unable to understand the contents of a document, does not provide proper identification, or appears to be under duress or coercion. Understanding when to refuse a notarization is just as important as knowing how to carry out a notarization, as it ensures that the process is legal and ethical.

As you continue in your role as a Notary Public, it's essential to keep your commission up to date. Your commission lasts for four years, and as the expiration date approaches, you will need to go through the renewal process to maintain your standing. The renewal process is similar to the initial commissioning process, but it may be less involved if you have maintained a clean record and have kept up with the necessary education requirements.

The commissioning process in California is a rigorous but rewarding path that helps ensure only qualified individuals are entrusted with the responsibility of notarizing documents. By following the steps outlined above, you can become a trusted and effective Notary Public, providing valuable services to your community while adhering to the laws and ethical standards of California.

# CHAPTER 2
## NOTARY PUBLIC LAWS AND REGULATIONS

### UNDERSTANDING CALIFORNIA NOTARY LAWS

Understanding California Notary Laws is a critical component of your role as a Notary Public. These laws are in place to guide Notaries in carrying out their responsibilities with accuracy and integrity. In California, the Notary Public serves a unique and essential role in safeguarding the public by verifying identities, preventing fraud, and ensuring that legal documents are properly executed. By fully understanding the intricacies of California's Notary laws, you can ensure that you perform your duties in accordance with the law and in a manner that inspires trust and confidence in the people you serve.

The foundation of California's Notary laws is built on the California Government Code, specifically Section 8200 through 8230. This body of law provides the rules and regulations that Notaries must follow when performing their duties. While it's vital to read and familiarize yourself with these laws in their entirety, it's also helpful to focus on some of the key aspects that define the role and responsibilities of a Notary Public in California.

One of the primary functions of a Notary Public in California is to verify the identity of individuals signing documents. The California Notary laws require Notaries to ensure that the person appearing before them is indeed the person they claim to be. This is done by reviewing government-issued identification such as a driver's license or passport. California Notaries are also responsible for ensuring that the signer understands the document they are signing and is not under any form of duress or coercion. This is a key part of the Notary's role in preventing fraud and ensuring that documents are signed willingly and knowingly.

In California, a Notary is also responsible for ensuring that all notarial acts are properly documented. This is where the use of a Notary journal comes into play. According to California law, every Notary Public must keep a journal of every notarial act performed. This journal is a legal record that includes essential information such as the date and time of the notarization, the type of document being notarized, the name of the signer, the method of identification used, and any other relevant details. The journal helps ensure accountability and serves as a vital tool if a question arises regarding the validity of a notarization. It's important to note that the journal must be kept in a secure location and should never be altered. In California, the journal is a public record and must be retained for at least 10 years after the date of the last notarization recorded in it.

While notarizing documents, a Notary in California must also be mindful of the legal requirements surrounding the types of documents that can and cannot be notarized. For example, the law is clear that a Notary Public in California cannot notarize a document in which they have a direct financial or beneficial interest. This means that you cannot notarize a document in which you, your spouse, or a close relative stand to gain financially. This rule is in place to avoid any potential conflict of interest and to ensure that Notaries act in the best interest of the public without personal gain influencing their actions.

One of the most important aspects of California Notary laws is the requirement for Notaries to maintain an impartial stance during the notarization process. This impartiality ensures that the Notary's role remains strictly to serve as an impartial witness, free from any bias. Notaries must avoid becoming involved in the content of the document being notarized and should not offer legal advice or assist in drafting or completing the document. This is a common misunderstanding among new Notaries, who may feel inclined to help the signer understand the document's contents or answer legal questions. However, California law prohibits such actions, as only licensed attorneys are authorized to provide legal advice. By refraining from offering legal guidance, Notaries ensure that they remain within the bounds of the law and protect themselves from potential liability.

Another important area to understand is the distinction between different types of notarizations. In California, there are primarily two types of notarizations that Notaries are asked to perform: an acknowledgment and a jurat. An *acknowledgment* is used when the signer is confirming that they signed the document voluntarily and with full understanding of its contents. This is typically used for documents such as deeds, powers of attorney, and other legal documents where the signer's intent and voluntary signature are important. On the other hand, a *jurat* is used when the signer swears or affirms that the contents of a document are true and correct. This is often used for affidavits, oaths, and other declarations made under penalty of perjury. It's important for a Notary to know the difference between these two types of notarizations, as each requires different steps and documentation.

One key aspect of California Notary law that is often overlooked is the handling of *oaths and affirmations*. While oaths are generally used for individuals who swear an oath on a religious text (such as the Bible), affirmations are a non-religious alternative for individuals who prefer to make a statement of truth without using a religious text. In California, Notaries must be aware of both types of declarations and ensure that the appropriate method is used based on the signer's preference. This is an important consideration, as it demonstrates respect for the signer's beliefs while also adhering to the law.

Another area of California Notary law that Notaries must be vigilant about is identifying situations where notarizations must be refused. California law provides clear guidelines for when a Notary is required to refuse a notarization. For example, if a signer cannot provide acceptable identification, or if they appear to be coerced, confused, or under duress, the Notary must refuse to perform the notarization. Additionally, if the Notary has any reason to believe that the signer does not understand the contents of the document, they are also required to refuse the notarization. This is crucial in maintaining the integrity of the notarization process and preventing fraudulent or coerced signatures.

It's also important to understand that California Notary laws are constantly evolving to meet new needs and address emerging concerns in the field of notarization. For example, California has made significant strides in adopting *electronic notarization* or *e-notarization*, allowing Notaries to perform notarizations remotely through digital platforms. While traditional notarizations are still the most common, e-notarization provides a flexible option for clients who are unable to be physically present in California. However, not all Notaries are authorized to perform e-notarizations, and special training and certification may be required to do so. Understanding the rules surrounding e-notarization and the technology involved is essential for Notaries who wish to take advantage of this growing trend.

Lastly, a critical aspect of California Notary laws is the penalties associated with non-compliance. Notaries who fail to follow the rules and regulations set forth by the California Secretary of State may face severe consequences, including fines, civil lawsuits, and the suspension or revocation of their Notary commission. For example, Notaries who knowingly perform fraudulent notarizations or who fail to keep proper records may be subject to criminal charges. It's vital for every Notary to take their role seriously and ensure that they comply with all applicable laws to protect both themselves and the public.

By understanding California Notary laws in detail, you are not only ensuring that you comply with the law but also positioning yourself to be a reliable, knowledgeable, and trusted Notary Public. Whether you are new to the profession or looking to refresh your knowledge, understanding the legal framework that governs your work is key to performing your duties with confidence and professionalism.

## RECENT LEGISLATIVE UPDATES AFFECTING NOTARIES

Recent legislative updates have a significant impact on the work of Notaries in California. These updates aim to address evolving needs, improve efficiency, and ensure that the Notary profession remains a trusted and reliable means of authenticating documents in a legal context. It's crucial for every Notary Public to stay informed about these changes to remain in compliance with the law, and to maintain the trust and integrity that come with the role. As new laws are introduced, or existing ones are amended, the responsibilities and best practices for Notaries also shift, requiring constant adaptation.

One of the most important recent legislative updates in California involves the expansion of *remote online notarization* (RON), a practice that was introduced during the COVID-19 pandemic. With the rise of digital platforms and remote transactions, California law has made provisions to accommodate the increasing demand for online notarizations. Remote notarization allows a Notary to notarize a document for a signer who is located anywhere in the world, as long as both parties are connected via video conferencing technology. This process includes verifying the signer's identity through online means, such as digital signatures and video verification. The law has evolved to make remote notarization a permanent practice in California, with specific rules about the use of technology and the security protocols that must be followed.

California has implemented stringent requirements for remote online notarizations to ensure that the integrity of the notarization process is maintained.

# California Notary Handbook 2025

Notaries who wish to conduct RON must undergo specialized training and register with an approved technology provider. This provider ensures that the Notary's electronic signature and seal are valid and legally recognized. Moreover, the Notary must follow security protocols to verify the identity of the signer, such as using multi-factor authentication and ensuring that the video conferencing tool used is secure. The law also mandates that the Notary record the entire notarization session, including both video and audio, which must be retained for a minimum of 10 years. This legislation is particularly relevant for Notaries who wish to provide services in an increasingly digital world and is an important example of how California is adapting its laws to meet the demands of a changing society.

Another significant change that has come with recent legislative updates in California is the regulation of *notarial journals*. Previously, Notaries were required to keep journals of their notarizations, but the details and methods for doing so were somewhat vague. However, new legislative updates have provided clear guidelines about how these journals should be maintained and what information must be recorded. In particular, the law now mandates that Notaries record the signer's *address* and *the type of document* being notarized. Additionally, the law requires Notaries to record a description of the identification presented by the signer, including the type of ID and its number. These updates were implemented to improve accountability and ensure that there is a clear, documented record of every notarization. These journals are not only a vital record for the Notary but also serve as an important legal tool in case of disputes or challenges to the notarization's validity.

Notaries in California must also be aware of *changes to fees* and the way fees are structured. California law has recently updated the maximum allowable fees that Notaries can charge for various types of notarizations. For example, Notaries can charge up to $15 for most notarizations, but this fee can vary depending on the type of service. The law now specifically outlines the circumstances in which a Notary may charge additional fees, such as for travel or for notarizing multiple documents at once. Notaries are required to provide a *written statement of fees* to the signer before performing a notarization, which ensures transparency and helps prevent misunderstandings. Keeping up to date with these changes is essential, as charging the wrong fee or failing to disclose fees correctly could result in penalties and damage to the Notary's professional reputation.

One notable legislative change concerns *notarial acts for specific types of documents*, especially in real estate transactions. California law has recently expanded the scope of documents that require a Notary's involvement, particularly in relation to *deeds, mortgages, and powers of attorney*. For instance, real estate transactions in California often require Notaries to notarize signatures on property transfer documents, such as deeds of trust or quitclaim deeds. The new laws governing these types of documents have set out more detailed instructions regarding the verification of the signer's identity and the specific requirements for notarization. Additionally, Notaries are now required to be more cautious when notarizing documents involving powers of attorney, ensuring that the signer has a clear understanding of the powers being granted and is acting voluntarily.

Recent updates have also introduced more detailed regulations regarding *acceptance of electronic documents*. As more legal documents move online, Notaries are increasingly being asked to notarize electronic versions of documents. While this has been allowed in California for some time, recent changes have strengthened the rules around electronic notarizations. The law now mandates that all electronic documents must be signed with a *secure electronic signature*, which must meet the California Secretary of State's standards for authenticity. Notaries performing electronic notarizations must use an approved technology platform that ensures the signature is not only authentic but also tamper-evident. The platform must be secure, and the Notary is responsible for ensuring that the platform meets all of California's regulatory requirements. These changes are designed to maintain the security and legality of electronic notarizations, and they provide a clearer framework for Notaries who perform these types of services.

One of the more subtle, yet important, legislative changes involves *notarial errors and penalties*. As a Notary, you are responsible for ensuring that all notarial acts are performed correctly, and recent laws have made it clear that errors in notarization are no longer taken lightly. The law has increased penalties for common mistakes, such as failing to properly complete the notarial certificate or failing to accurately record the details of the notarization in the journal. Notaries can now face civil penalties and fines if they are found to have failed in these areas. Additionally, Notaries who fail to maintain their journals or who fail to provide proper records when requested could face more severe penalties, including suspension or revocation of their commission. This underscores the importance of diligence and attention to detail in every notarial act, ensuring that you follow the procedures outlined by law every time you notarize a document.

In addition to these significant updates, California has introduced new requirements for *Notary education and training*. California law mandates that Notaries complete a specific amount of education and training before being commissioned, and recent updates have refined these requirements. Notaries are required to take a state-approved training course before taking the Notary exam. The course must cover essential topics, including notarial procedures, ethical guidelines, and the laws governing notarization in California. Furthermore, Notaries are required to complete additional continuing education every few years to maintain their commission. This is designed to ensure that Notaries remain knowledgeable about changes in the law and continue to meet the high standards of practice that the public and the legal system expect from them.

Finally, one of the most recent and impactful legislative changes concerns *identity theft and fraud prevention*. California has made significant strides in strengthening its laws surrounding the prevention of identity theft. As a Notary Public, you play a crucial role in preventing fraudulent activity, particularly when it comes to verifying the identity of signers. In response to rising concerns over identity theft, recent updates to the law require Notaries to take additional steps to verify the identity of individuals. This includes accepting only certain forms of identification, ensuring that the identification is current, and in some cases, using more advanced methods such as biometric verification or online identity checks for remote notarizations. Notaries must also be aware of the *suspected fraudulent activities* and know when to refuse a notarization if they have any doubt about the legitimacy of the signer or the document.

The recent legislative updates affecting Notaries in California are designed to address the growing complexity of notarization and to ensure that Notaries can continue to serve as a reliable safeguard in legal and business transactions. These updates are not just about keeping up with technological advancements but also about ensuring that Notaries maintain their trustworthiness, professionalism, and attention to detail. By staying informed about these changes and adapting to the new rules and regulations, Notaries can continue to provide valuable services to the public while avoiding potential pitfalls and legal issues. Understanding these legislative updates is vital for any Notary who wants to remain compliant with California law and provide the highest standard of service to their clients.

## AUTHORIZED NOTARIAL ACTS AND THEIR LEGAL IMPLICATIONS

Authorized notarial acts are at the very core of the responsibilities entrusted to a Notary Public in California. Each act a Notary performs has significant legal implications, not only for the parties involved but also for the integrity of the legal system itself. Understanding what actions a Notary is authorized to perform and how these actions are governed by law is crucial for any aspiring or practicing Notary Public. Notaries in California are empowered to carry out specific tasks that ensure the authenticity and reliability of documents, whether for legal, business, or personal use. It is important to understand both the scope and limits of these powers, as well as the legal consequences of performing these acts incorrectly or outside of the legal boundaries.

The most commonly recognized notarial acts that a Notary is authorized to perform in California are *acknowledgments*, *oaths and affirmations*, *jurats*, *copy certifications*, and *protests*. Each of these acts serves a different purpose, and it is essential for Notaries to know the specific procedures for each. By understanding these acts, you will not only be able to accurately fulfill your duties but also avoid common pitfalls that could lead to liability or even the revocation of your commission.

An *acknowledgment* is one of the most common notarial acts and involves the Notary confirming that the signer of a document has appeared before them, acknowledged that they signed the document voluntarily, and that they were properly identified. In California, the signer must appear in person before the Notary, and the Notary must confirm the identity of the signer through acceptable identification, such as a driver's license or passport. If the signer is a corporate officer or other authorized representative, the Notary must confirm their authority to act on behalf of the organization. The Notary will then verify that the signature on the document is genuine, the signer's actions were voluntary, and that the signer understands the document's contents. The legal implications of an acknowledgment are that it provides a foundation of authenticity and assurance that the document has been signed intentionally and with understanding.

A *jurat*, in contrast, is a notarial act that requires the Notary to verify that the signer has taken an oath or affirmation to swear or affirm that the contents of the document are true. This is often used in affidavits, depositions, and other legal documents where the signer attests to the truthfulness of the information contained in the document. In California, the signer must take an oath or affirmation in the presence of the Notary, and the Notary must confirm the signer's identity, typically by reviewing acceptable identification. Once the oath or affirmation is taken, the Notary will complete the jurat by signing and affixing their seal to the document. The legal implication of a jurat is that it makes the statement in the document legally binding. If the information provided by the signer is false, the signer may be subject to penalties for perjury. The importance of this act cannot be overstated, as it serves to ensure that individuals are held accountable for the truthfulness of their statements.

An *oath* or *affirmation* is another key notarial act. An oath requires the signer to swear to tell the truth, typically by invoking a religious or personal belief. An affirmation is similar but is a secular declaration that does not require any religious reference. Both acts carry the legal weight of making the statement or document legally binding. As with a jurat, the Notary must verify the identity of the signer before the oath or affirmation is administered. If a person is found to have made a false statement under oath, they could be subject to serious legal consequences, including charges of perjury. The act of swearing an oath or making an affirmation holds individuals accountable for their words and actions, and this responsibility is one that a Notary facilitates with great care.

Another important authorized notarial act is *copy certification*. This involves the Notary certifying that a copy of an original document is a true and accurate reproduction. It is important to note that in California, Notaries are only authorized to certify copies of certain types of documents. For example, Notaries are not allowed to certify copies of vital records, such as birth, death, or marriage certificates, unless specifically authorized by law. In order to certify a copy, the Notary must compare the original document with the copy, confirm that they are identical, and then sign and seal the copy to affirm its authenticity. The legal implication of a certified copy is that it provides assurance that the copy is an exact duplicate of the original document, and it may be used in lieu of the original for various legal or business purposes. However, the Notary's certification does not verify the truth or accuracy of the content of the original document; it only attests to the fact that the copy is a faithful reproduction.

In the realm of finance and banking, Notaries are also often called upon to perform *protests* for non-payment of negotiable instruments, such as promissory notes or checks. A *protest* is a formal declaration by the Notary that a document has been presented for payment and that payment has been refused. In California, the protest is typically used when a negotiable instrument, like a check, is presented for payment but is not honored by the bank. The Notary will record the facts surrounding the non-payment, such as the date, time, and circumstances of the refusal. This notarial act is significant because it can be used as evidence in legal proceedings if the matter progresses to litigation. A protest serves as a formal record of the fact that payment was not made and is often used in financial disputes, particularly in situations where there is a need to establish that payment was due but not received.

While these are some of the most common notarial acts, it is important to understand that Notaries in California are not authorized to perform every act that might be requested of them. For example, Notaries are not authorized to give legal advice, even if they are asked about the content of the document being notarized. The role of a Notary is limited to verifying identities, administering oaths, witnessing signatures, and performing other specified acts within the boundaries of the law. Providing legal advice or engaging in activities that could be construed as practicing law could result in serious legal consequences for the Notary. This is an essential distinction that all Notaries must keep in mind. A Notary's primary role is to provide a service that ensures the integrity of documents and transactions, not to interpret or guide others on the content of those documents.

The legal implications of performing a notarial act incorrectly or beyond the scope of authority are significant. If a Notary performs an act in violation of California law, they could face fines, civil penalties, or even the revocation of their commission. In some cases, the Notary may be held liable for damages if their mistake causes harm to another party. For example, if a Notary fails to verify a signer's identity properly and the document is later found to be fraudulent, the Notary could be held responsible for the error, even though they may not have intended to facilitate the fraud. Additionally, performing an unauthorized act could result in criminal charges if the Notary is found to be intentionally violating the law.

One example of an unauthorized act could be notarizing a document in which the Notary has a direct interest. This is strictly prohibited in California, as it could lead to a conflict of interest. Notaries must avoid situations where they could stand to gain personally from the notarization, as this could compromise the integrity of the act. Furthermore, notarizing documents without the signer's presence or without proper identification is another violation that can carry severe legal consequences.

Understanding the scope of authorized notarial acts and their legal implications is fundamental for any Notary. Each act performed carries legal weight, and it is essential to ensure that you are acting within the boundaries of the law. By familiarizing yourself with the specific notarial acts you are authorized to perform and the legal ramifications of your actions, you can fulfill your duties with confidence and professionalism. In doing so, you will help ensure the continued trust and reliability of the notarization process in California.

## PROHIBITED ACTS AND COMMON LEGAL PITFALLS

As a Notary Public in California, understanding what you are prohibited from doing is just as important as knowing what you are authorized to do. Violating the rules governing notarial acts can result in serious legal consequences, including civil penalties, the loss of your commission, and even criminal charges. Notaries play an essential role in maintaining the integrity of legal and financial documents, and with this responsibility comes the necessity to avoid prohibited acts and common legal pitfalls. Each misstep could have far-reaching effects, both for you as a Notary and for those relying on your services.

The first and perhaps most important rule to remember is that as a Notary Public, you are not authorized to give legal advice. Even if someone comes to you asking for guidance on the content or meaning of a document, you must politely refrain from offering any interpretation, explanation, or counsel regarding the document. The Notary's role is strictly to perform the notarial act—such as verifying the identity of the signer and witnessing their signature—not to provide insight into the document's legal implications. Doing so could result in the unauthorized practice of law, which is illegal and punishable under California law. It's important to emphasize that the line between providing a notarial service and giving legal advice can sometimes seem thin, especially when dealing with complex documents. However, any time you explain what a document means or suggest what action the signer should take, you are engaging in the unauthorized practice of law. If a signer requests assistance in understanding the document, it is appropriate to suggest that they consult an attorney.

Another prohibited act for a Notary Public in California is notarizing documents in which you have a personal interest. This includes notarizing a document in which you or your immediate family members have a financial stake or benefit. Such an action could create a conflict of interest, impairing your ability to be impartial. For example, if a Notary is asked to notarize a contract in which they are a party, this would be a clear violation of California law. California law is explicit in stating that a Notary must not notarize documents in which they are personally involved. By doing so, a Notary would be opening themselves up to accusations of fraud or bias, undermining the trust that is essential to the notarial process. The goal of a Notary is to be a neutral third party—acting only as a witness to the signing and verifying the authenticity of the signature and the identity of the signer. Whenever you have a direct interest in the outcome of the notarized document, you should immediately decline to perform the notarization.

Along the same lines, it is prohibited for a Notary Public in California to notarize a document in which the signer is not physically present before them at the time of notarization. This rule is crucial for maintaining the integrity of the notarization process. Notarization is a solemn act, and the purpose of the Notary's role is to verify the identity of the signer, witness their signature, and ensure that the signer is acting voluntarily and under no duress. If the signer is not physically present, the Notary cannot fulfill these essential responsibilities. Notarizing a document without the signer being present, sometimes referred to as "remote notarization" or "notarizing by proxy," is strictly prohibited under California law, unless specific provisions are made by the state to allow such actions in the future. As of now, in-person notarizations remain a requirement for any official notarization.

In addition, Notaries in California are prohibited from performing notarizations if they are unsure of the identity of the signer. Verifying the identity of the signer is one of the fundamental responsibilities of a Notary Public. California law requires that the signer provide satisfactory evidence of their identity, such as a valid driver's license or passport. If a Notary is unsure or unable to confirm the identity of the signer, they must refuse to perform the notarization. This helps to safeguard against identity fraud and ensures that documents are being notarized by the rightful individual. Notaries should be familiar with the forms of identification that are considered acceptable by California law and must also be able to recognize and address any red flags when presented with suspicious identification.

Another common legal pitfall for Notaries involves *improperly completing the notarial certificate*. A notarial certificate is the statement the Notary attaches to the document being notarized, and it provides the legal context for the notarization. It typically includes the Notary's signature, seal, the date, the venue (location), and the type of notarial act performed, such as an acknowledgment or jurat. An improper or incomplete certificate can render a notarization invalid. For example, if the Notary fails to include the venue or the correct date, it could be questioned in court, leading to potential challenges to the validity of the notarized document. A common issue arises when a Notary mistakenly uses the wrong certificate for a particular act. For example, using an acknowledgment certificate when a jurat should be used, or vice versa, can result in confusion and even the rejection of the notarized document. The proper completion of the notarial certificate is essential for ensuring that the notarization is legally recognized and effective.

One of the most common legal pitfalls is notarizing a document that has been altered after it was signed by the individual. Altering a notarized document after it has been signed can seriously undermine its legal validity. A Notary must refuse to notarize a document that shows signs of being altered or tampered with in any way. If a document has been altered after the signer's original signature has been placed, the Notary should not perform the notarization, as this could expose them to liability. In the event that a notarized document is later found to have been altered, it could lead to questions about the Notary's role in the process, and the Notary could face penalties, including the loss of their commission. The Notary must ensure that the document being notarized is in its final form and has not been altered after the signer has executed it.

Additionally, Notaries must be cautious when dealing with *incomplete documents*. Notaries should never notarize documents that are incomplete or blank in sections that should contain information. For example, notarizing a document that has blanks in crucial areas, such as the date, amount of a financial transaction, or the name of the parties involved, is not only risky but also a violation of California notary law. Incomplete documents raise concerns about potential fraud, as the missing information could be filled in after the notarization. If you are presented with an incomplete document, you should either refuse to notarize it or ensure that it is fully completed before proceeding with the notarial act.

Notarizing a document without the signer's *voluntary* consent is another violation that can lead to serious legal consequences. If there is any indication that the signer is under duress, coercion, or threat while signing, you must refuse to notarize the document. California law is clear about the importance of ensuring that the signer is acting freely and without pressure when executing the document. A Notary should be vigilant for signs of duress, which might include the signer appearing fearful, intimidated, or being unable to explain the document's contents. If there are concerns about the signer's willingness to sign, you must not proceed with the notarization.

Finally, one of the most common legal pitfalls is neglecting to maintain proper records of your notarial acts. California law requires Notaries to keep a journal of all notarial acts performed. Failure to maintain this journal, or failure to accurately record the details of each notarization, can lead to fines, penalties, or even revocation of your commission. The journal should include the date and time of the notarization, a description of the document, the names of the parties involved, the type of notarial act performed, and the type of identification used to verify the signer's identity. Keeping an accurate and thorough journal is not only a legal requirement but also a good practice that can protect you in the event of a dispute or investigation.

Each of these prohibited acts and legal pitfalls serves as a reminder of the importance of performing your duties as a Notary Public with the utmost care and integrity. By understanding the boundaries of your role and adhering to the rules set forth by California law, you will help ensure that your notarizations are legally valid and recognized. It is vital that you remain vigilant, continue to educate yourself about the laws governing notarizations, and always strive to perform your duties in a way that upholds the trust placed in you as a Notary Public.

# CHAPTER 3
## NOTARIAL ACTS AND PROCEDURES

### ACKNOWLEDGMENTS

An *acknowledgment* is one of the most common and vital notarial acts a Notary Public performs in California. It is crucial to understand the purpose, procedures, and specific requirements surrounding acknowledgments in order to carry out your duties as a Notary properly and in full compliance with California law. The acknowledgment serves a significant role in authenticating documents for use in legal and financial transactions. As a Notary, you must have a comprehensive understanding of how acknowledgments work and how they should be handled to ensure that the notarization is both legally binding and valid.

The purpose of an acknowledgment is to verify the identity of the signer of a document and to confirm that the signer is willingly and knowingly signing the document. The signer must also acknowledge that they understand the content of the document, although the Notary is not responsible for explaining or interpreting the contents of the document. The *acknowledgment* is typically used in legal, financial, and real estate transactions, where it is important to ensure that the document has been signed by the right person, and that the signature is made voluntarily and without coercion. Common examples of documents requiring an acknowledgment include deeds, powers of attorney, contracts, and affidavits. The acknowledgment ensures that these documents will be recognized as valid in a court of law or by any institution relying on them.

In the context of the notarial act, when someone asks for an acknowledgment, it is essentially an assurance that the signer is appearing before the Notary and is the person they claim to be. However, the Notary is not responsible for verifying the truthfulness of the contents of the document itself; they are merely certifying the identity of the signer and ensuring that the signature was made voluntarily. This is an important distinction because a Notary cannot be held responsible for the actions or decisions of the signer in relation to the content of the document.

To perform an acknowledgment in California, the signer must appear in person before the Notary and must personally acknowledge their signature. The signer must also be able to present valid identification that satisfies the Notary's requirement for proving their identity. California law allows for various forms of identification, such as a state-issued driver's license, passport, or other government-issued IDs. It is important that the Notary closely examines the identification to ensure that it is current, valid, and matches the person before them. If the Notary has any doubts about the identity of the signer, the acknowledgment cannot be performed, and the Notary must refuse to notarize the document. The Notary should be diligent in ensuring that they are not inadvertently committing an act of fraud by notarizing a document for someone whose identity they cannot verify.

Once the signer's identity has been confirmed, the Notary will proceed with completing the notarial certificate, which is the official statement that accompanies the notarized document. For an acknowledgment, the notarial certificate must include several essential elements: the Notary's name and title, the venue (location of the notarization), the date of the acknowledgment, the signature of the Notary, the type of document being notarized, and the details confirming that the signer acknowledged their signature. It is important to understand that the certificate must be filled out completely and accurately. Missing or incomplete information in the certificate can render the notarization invalid. For instance, leaving out the venue or the date could cause a court or another institution to question the authenticity of the document.

When performing an acknowledgment, the Notary must ensure that the document is *fully completed* before notarizing it. It is illegal to notarize a document that is incomplete, as this raises concerns about potential fraud. An acknowledgment requires the signer to confirm that they are signing a document voluntarily, with full awareness of its contents, and without any form of duress. If the document is incomplete or has blanks, the Notary cannot proceed with the acknowledgment. For example, if a document requires the amount of money in a financial agreement to be filled in, the Notary cannot notarize it unless that section is properly completed.

Another key element of the acknowledgment process is the *voluntariness* of the signer. The signer must sign the document of their own free will, without any duress or coercion. If at any point the Notary believes the signer is being forced to sign the document, or if the Notary suspects that the signer is under duress, they must refuse to notarize the document. The signer must be of sound mind and acting voluntarily, and it is the Notary's responsibility to assess these conditions before proceeding. If the signer appears to be coerced, the Notary should immediately halt the notarial act and explain that notarization cannot proceed under those circumstances. A failure to identify signs of duress could expose the Notary to legal consequences and would compromise the legitimacy of the notarization.

Notaries must also be cautious when dealing with individuals who may not fully understand the document they are signing. While the Notary is not tasked with explaining the content of the document, they are responsible for ensuring that the signer understands they are acknowledging their signature. For instance, if a signer is illiterate or has limited understanding of the language of the document, it is advisable for the Notary to recommend that the signer seek guidance from an attorney or another professional who can explain the document's contents. The Notary should refrain from providing any explanation about the document itself but may ask the signer if they fully understand the nature of the document. If the signer expresses confusion or uncertainty, the Notary should not proceed with the acknowledgment.

Once the signer has acknowledged their signature and the document has been completed, the Notary will affix their seal and signature to the notarial certificate. The *seal* is an essential tool in notarization, as it serves as a mark of authenticity and legality. The seal should be applied securely and should clearly display the Notary's name and commission number. The seal should not be affixed to any document unless it has been completed according to the proper procedures. The Notary should also ensure that their signature on the certificate is legible and placed in the correct section. It is important that the Notary does not rush through the notarial act; every step should be completed with precision and care to avoid mistakes that could invalidate the notarization or cause confusion later.

The completion of the acknowledgment also includes making sure the appropriate journal entry is made. In California, Notaries are required to keep a journal of all notarial acts they perform, and this includes acknowledgments. A proper journal entry should document the name of the signer, the date and time of the acknowledgment, the type of document being notarized, the type of identification presented, and any relevant details that would assist in verifying the legitimacy of the notarization. It is a legal requirement to maintain an accurate journal, and failure to do so can result in penalties or the revocation of the Notary's commission. Maintaining a thorough record of your notarial acts is not only a safeguard for you but also a protection for the parties involved in the notarization.

A common question that arises in the context of acknowledgments is whether the Notary can notarize a document in which they have a personal interest. The answer is no—Notaries are prohibited from notarizing documents in which they have a financial or personal stake. For example, if a Notary is involved in a transaction where they stand to gain financially from the document, they must refrain from performing the acknowledgment. This rule helps prevent conflicts of interest and ensures that the Notary acts impartially, as the role of the Notary is to remain a neutral third party. If you find yourself in a situation where there may be a conflict of interest, it is important to step aside and let another Notary handle the matter.

Understanding the procedure for an acknowledgment, following the proper steps, and adhering to the legal requirements is essential for performing a valid notarial act in California. By staying mindful of the regulations governing acknowledgments, you can help ensure that your notarial services are of the highest quality and that the documents you notarize will be legally accepted and recognized. Always remember that as a Notary Public, your role is to safeguard the integrity of the notarization process, acting as a neutral witness and ensuring that the signer is properly identified and acting of their own free will.

## JURATS

A *jurat* is one of the most significant and frequently encountered notarial acts that a Notary Public will perform. In California, as in many other jurisdictions, the purpose of a jurat is to administer an oath or affirmation to a signer who is swearing to the truthfulness of the contents of a document. Jurats are primarily used for affidavits and other documents where the signer must swear under penalty of perjury that the information contained in the document is true and correct. Understanding the procedure, requirements, and responsibilities associated with administering a jurat is essential for any Notary looking to perform their duties with accuracy and professionalism.

A jurat differs from an acknowledgment in that it specifically requires the signer to take an oath or affirmation. In an acknowledgment, the signer simply acknowledges their signature on a document, confirming that it was signed voluntarily and without coercion. In contrast, with a jurat, the signer swears or affirms that the contents of the document are true, and the Notary serves as the officer who administers the oath or affirmation. The key element in a jurat is that the signer is swearing to the truth of the statements in the document, and by doing so, they are subject to penalties for perjury if the statements are false.

The first and most crucial requirement for performing a jurat is that the signer must be physically present before the Notary. Unlike an acknowledgment, where the signer must simply acknowledge their signature, a jurat involves taking an oath or affirmation. It is imperative that the signer is not only present, but also fully aware of the significance of the act they are about to undertake. The signer must understand that by taking the oath or affirmation, they are legally committing to the truthfulness of the contents of the document, and any false statement may result in criminal charges for perjury.

When administering a jurat, the Notary must ensure that the signer fully comprehends the document they are swearing to, although the Notary is not required to explain its content. The Notary is responsible for ensuring that the signer is swearing or affirming to the truth of the document in a legal capacity, but it is the signer's responsibility to understand the content and to ensure that the document reflects accurate information. For example, if a signer is not familiar with the language of the document or has difficulty understanding it, the Notary should recommend that they seek assistance from a professional, such as an attorney, to interpret the document for them. It is not the Notary's role to explain the contents of the document, but the Notary must ensure that the signer has the capacity to take the oath or affirmation.

Once the signer is prepared to take the oath or affirmation, the Notary will ask them to swear or affirm that the contents of the document are true. An oath is a formal declaration that the signer is swearing by a higher power (e.g., God) that the information in the document is truthful. An affirmation, on the other hand, is a solemn declaration made without reference to a higher power, and it is often used by individuals who have religious or personal objections to swearing an oath. California law allows both oaths and affirmations, and the Notary must ensure that the signer's choice of method is respected. The Notary should make the signer aware that they are choosing to swear or affirm the truthfulness of the document before they proceed with either option.

After the signer has taken the oath or affirmation, the Notary must complete the *jurat certificate*, which is the official statement that accompanies the notarized document. The jurat certificate should include specific information to validate the notarial act. This includes the Notary's name, commission number, and title, as well as the venue (the location of the notarization). The certificate must also indicate that the signer appeared before the Notary, took an oath or affirmation, and swore or affirmed the truthfulness of the document. The date of the jurat must be included, and the Notary must sign and affix their seal to the certificate.

Without a completed jurat certificate, the notarization will be incomplete and may not hold up in a legal setting.

One important thing to note is that the document being sworn to must be fully completed before the Notary administers the jurat. A Notary may not notarize a document that contains blanks or is incomplete in any way. This is especially true for documents such as affidavits, where the signer's statement is at the core of the document's validity. For example, if an affidavit states a certain fact but leaves spaces for the facts to be filled in, the Notary cannot administer the jurat until those blanks are properly filled in. This ensures that the signer is swearing to the entirety of the document, and that the document will be clear and complete when it is presented for legal or official purposes.

Additionally, the Notary must carefully verify the identity of the signer before proceeding with the jurat. California law requires the Notary to personally identify the signer and ensure that they are who they claim to be. This typically involves presenting a valid government-issued identification card, such as a driver's license, passport, or other acceptable forms of ID. The Notary should closely examine the identification for authenticity, ensuring it is current, not expired, and free from any signs of tampering. If the Notary has any doubts about the signer's identity, they must refuse to administer the jurat. It is critical that the Notary ensures they are performing their duties with integrity and upholds the trust placed in them by the public.

The administration of a jurat also involves an important consideration regarding the *language* of the document. If the signer cannot understand the language in which the document is written, it is up to the signer to arrange for translation or explanation of the document. The Notary is not responsible for translating documents or providing an explanation of their content, but the signer must have a clear understanding that they are swearing to the truthfulness of the document. If the Notary is not confident that the signer fully understands the document, it is a good practice to stop the notarization and ask the signer to seek additional help. Any confusion or misunderstanding on the part of the signer can lead to problems later on, especially if the document is used in a legal dispute.

Once the Notary has completed the jurat certificate, affixed their seal, and signed the document, the notarization is complete. However, the Notary must not forget one crucial element—*recordkeeping*. California law requires Notaries to maintain a journal of all notarial acts they perform, including jurats. The journal entry for a jurat must include the name of the signer, the type of document, the date and time of the notarization, and a description of the ID used by the signer. The Notary should make the journal entry in a clear and accurate manner to ensure a reliable record of the notarization. The journal serves as an essential tool for the Notary, as it provides documentation in case the notarization is ever called into question. Keeping a well-maintained journal is a key component of ensuring that the Notary is complying with all applicable laws and maintaining a high standard of professionalism.

Finally, it is important to note that Notaries are prohibited from performing a jurat on documents in which they have a personal interest. This is an ethical standard that helps prevent conflicts of interest and ensures the Notary's impartiality. If a Notary has a personal stake in the content or outcome of the document being sworn to, they should refuse to perform the jurat. For example, if the signer is a family member or business partner, or if the Notary stands to gain financially from the contents of the document, they must step aside and allow another Notary to complete the task. Performing notarizations with integrity is essential to maintaining the public's trust in the notarial profession.

In administering a jurat, the Notary plays a vital role in ensuring that documents are properly sworn to, are complete, and reflect the truth. The Notary must remain vigilant in adhering to the procedural and legal requirements that govern the notarial act, including confirming the identity of the signer, administering the oath or affirmation, and completing the jurat certificate accurately. By upholding these standards, the Notary not only ensures the validity of the notarized document but also contributes to the legal and professional integrity of the notarial system in California.

## OATHS AND AFFIRMATIONS

In the world of notarial acts, understanding the difference between oaths and affirmations, as well as how to administer each correctly, is essential. In California, notaries are called upon to administer both oaths and affirmations as part of their duties, often in the context of jurats, affidavits, and other legal documents. These two actions, while similar, have distinct legal and procedural differences that a notary must fully grasp in order to perform their role accurately and in accordance with the law.

An *oath* is a solemn declaration, typically made with reference to a higher power, in which the individual swears that the contents of a document are true. In many cases, individuals take an oath based on their religious beliefs, with the most common form being an oath taken "so help me God." The act of swearing an oath holds a certain level of gravity and seriousness, as it emphasizes that the individual is bound by their faith to tell the truth. It is commonly used in situations where the individual is swearing to the veracity of statements made in a document, such as in the case of an affidavit or deposition.

An *affirmation*, on the other hand, is a similar statement of truthfulness, but it does not involve a reference to a higher power. Instead, an affirmation is a secular statement in which the individual affirms under penalty of perjury that the information in the document is true. The language of an affirmation might sound something like "I affirm under penalty of perjury that the contents of this document are true and correct." This option is often provided for individuals who have a religious or personal objection to swearing an oath. It is a legally recognized method of making the same commitment to truthfulness as an oath, but without invoking religious beliefs.

For a notary public in California, both oaths and affirmations are legally valid methods of swearing to the truth of a statement. However, it is important for the notary to understand the distinction between the two and to administer them properly. Both require the signer to take a sworn statement about the truthfulness of a document, but the language and nature of the commitment differ. Notaries must be aware of the signer's preference and ensure that the correct form of declaration is administered based on the individual's beliefs and the legal requirements of the document.

When administering an *oath*, the notary's role is to administer the oath in accordance with the specific wording requested by the signer. Typically, the notary will ask the signer to raise their right hand and swear to the truth of the statements in the document, making the declaration "so help me God" or using a similar phrase depending on the circumstances. This process is formal, and the notary should ensure that the signer fully understands the gravity of the oath they are taking. The notary must also verify the signer's identity before proceeding with any notarial act, including oaths, to ensure the correct individual is taking the oath.

In contrast, administering an *affirmation* is similarly formal, but it excludes any religious language. The notary would ask the signer to affirm that the contents of the document are true and correct, using the appropriate legal phrasing. While the process is less tied to religious beliefs, it is equally important to ensure the signer understands the consequences of making a false statement under penalty of perjury. The notary should take care to clarify that an affirmation holds the same legal weight as an oath and that the signer is subject to the same penalties for falsehoods, including perjury charges.

One of the most important aspects of administering an oath or affirmation is making sure that the *language* used is clear and unequivocal. The notary is not required to explain the contents of the document, but they must confirm that the signer understands the implications of the statement they are making. In some cases, a signer may request a translation of the language of the oath or affirmation if they do not fully understand it. While a notary is not required to act as a translator, they must ensure that the signer is competent to take the oath or affirmation and should recommend the assistance of a translator or attorney if there are concerns about language barriers or comprehension.

Once the signer has taken the oath or affirmation, the notary must complete the notarial certificate, ensuring that it accurately reflects the method used. The notary will need to indicate whether the individual swore an oath or made an affirmation, as the two must be differentiated in the certificate. The notary should also sign the document, affix their seal, and include the venue and date. This notarial certificate serves as a record of the act performed and helps establish the validity of the document in question.

In some cases, a *jurat*, which involves both an oath or affirmation, is required. For example, an affidavit requires a jurat, where the signer must swear or affirm that the statements within the affidavit are true and correct. The notary will administer either an oath or an affirmation, depending on the signer's preference, and then complete the jurat certificate. The notary's role in administering a jurat is critical, as it not only ensures the signer is bound by their statement under penalty of perjury but also establishes the legal foundation for the document. It is imperative that the document be completed and signed before the notary administers the jurat, as the notary must only certify the contents of a fully completed document.

While performing the oath or affirmation, the notary must ensure that the signer is not under duress, coercion, or undue influence. The individual taking the oath or affirmation must do so voluntarily and with a full understanding of what they are committing to. If there is any indication that the signer is being pressured to sign the document, the notary must refuse to perform the notarial act. This protection ensures that the notary's role remains impartial and that the integrity of the notarial process is preserved.

California law does not permit a notary to administer an oath or affirmation to anyone who has a personal interest in the matter being sworn to. For example, a notary may not take an oath or affirmation from a family member, business partner, or anyone else who stands to gain from the document being sworn to. This rule helps prevent conflicts of interest and upholds the ethical standards of the notarial profession.

Moreover, there are certain types of documents and situations where a notary is prohibited from administering an oath or affirmation. For example, a notary may not administer an oath or affirmation in a manner that would result in perjury or other legal violations. If a notary has reason to believe that the signer is knowingly swearing to false information, the notary must refuse to administer the oath or affirmation. A notary must remain diligent and impartial, always acting in the best interests of the law and maintaining the public's trust in the notarial process.

In practice, notaries must remain mindful of the context in which they are asked to administer oaths and affirmations. For instance, when working with legal documents like affidavits, depositions, or court declarations, the notary must ensure that the signer understands the full legal weight of their statement and the possible consequences of perjury. The notary must also be mindful of any special circumstances, such as if the signer is in a foreign language or has a disability that affects their understanding of the document.

Proper administration of oaths and affirmations is a vital part of the notary public's role, as it ensures the integrity of documents and serves as a safeguard against fraudulent or false statements. Notaries must be well-versed in the legalities and requirements of both oaths and affirmations, ensuring that each is properly executed and that all necessary steps are followed in accordance with California law. By maintaining attention to detail, staying impartial, and acting with professionalism, notaries can contribute to a legal framework that relies on truthfulness and honesty, helping to preserve the integrity of legal transactions across the state.

## COPY CERTIFICATIONS

One of the many duties that a notary public in California may be asked to perform is certifying copies of documents. This notarial act is often misunderstood, yet it holds substantial importance in legal and business processes. As a notary, understanding the detailed guidelines, limitations, and protocols surrounding copy certifications is essential to ensuring that you are abiding by the law while providing a valuable service. Whether you're certifying copies of vital records, legal documents, or personal paperwork, you need to be fully aware of your responsibilities and the limits of your authority in this area.

In California, a notary public is authorized to certify copies of documents under certain conditions. However, not all documents can be certified. The role of the notary in copy certification is to attest that a copy is a true and accurate reproduction of an original document. Unlike other notarial acts such as acknowledgments, oaths, or jurats, the primary purpose of a copy certification is to confirm that the duplicate document exactly matches the original in both content and form.

Before delving into the details of how to perform copy certifications and the limits on this process, it's important to clarify the role of the notary. A notary is not tasked with determining the validity or legal sufficiency of the original document. Instead, the notary's duty is simply to verify that the copy is a true and faithful reproduction of the original document that was presented to them. The notary is not required to read the content of the document in detail, nor should they offer legal advice or attempt to interpret the document's meaning.

In California, the authority to perform copy certifications is governed by specific guidelines that notaries must adhere to. The most important thing to understand is that a notary may only certify copies of documents that the notary has personally witnessed. This means that the notary must have the original document in their possession when performing the certification. A copy certification cannot be performed if the notary has not personally examined the original document. Furthermore, the notary cannot certify copies of documents that were not originally signed by the person whose signature appears on the document, unless they are also the person requesting the certification.

It's important to note that California law prohibits notaries from certifying copies of certain types of documents. For example, a notary public in California is specifically prohibited from certifying copies of vital records such as birth certificates, death certificates, and marriage certificates. These types of documents must be obtained directly from the relevant government agency or authority, and only the agency itself can issue a certified copy. Notaries should be cautious when asked to certify such documents, as failing to adhere to the law could lead to legal consequences and even a loss of notary commission.

In addition to the restrictions on vital records, California law also prevents notaries from certifying copies of documents that are not original. For example, if a person presents a photocopy of a document instead of the original, the notary may not certify the photocopy as a true copy of the original. The law requires that the notary physically examine the original document before performing a certification. This ensures that the notary's role remains limited to verifying that a copy matches the original and does not extend to validating the content or legality of the original document.

Once the notary has examined the original document and verified that the copy matches it exactly, the process of certifying the copy can begin. To properly perform a copy certification, the notary must make a statement on the document certifying that the copy is a true and correct reproduction of the original. This certification must be included in a notarial certificate, which is a specific form that accompanies the certified copy. The notary's certificate should clearly indicate the following elements: that the copy is a true and correct copy of the original, that the notary has personally examined the original, and the date on which the certification was performed. The notary must also sign and stamp the certificate, just as they would with any other notarial act.

Notaries should be careful to avoid making any misleading or erroneous statements when certifying copies. For instance, notaries should never state that a document is "authentic" or "legally valid" when certifying a copy. The notary's role is solely to verify that the copy matches the original, not to vouch for the legal standing or authenticity of the document itself. Providing such misleading statements could expose the notary to liability or legal challenges. It is crucial that notaries maintain their impartiality and stick strictly to their role in the copy certification process.

Another important guideline to be aware of is that a notary is not authorized to certify copies of certain documents, even if those documents are not subject to the restrictions outlined above. For example, a notary cannot certify a copy of a document that they themselves have created, such as a notarized document with their own signature. The purpose of certification is to ensure that a document matches an original document that is independent of the notary's involvement. This rule ensures that there is no conflict of interest in the certification process.

Notaries should also be aware that the recipient of a certified copy may need to present additional documentation or proof of the validity of the original document. In some cases, even when a document is certified by a notary, the receiving party may request further verification or legal authentication, especially if the document will be used in court or for international purposes. Notaries should never attempt to provide additional documentation or validation of the original document's legality, as that falls outside the scope of their role.

There are some common situations where individuals might request certified copies, and understanding these scenarios can help notaries prepare for such requests. For instance, when individuals are applying for immigration or visa purposes, they may need certified copies of documents such as birth certificates, marriage certificates, or court orders. In such cases, the notary's role is to certify that the copy matches the original document, but the notary should never assume responsibility for the contents or legal validity of the document. Notaries should always be clear with clients about the limits of their authority in these instances.

One critical limitation to keep in mind is that notaries cannot certify copies of any document that has been altered or tampered with in any way. If the original document has been altered or if there are signs of tampering, the notary cannot certify the copy. Notaries should closely examine the original document for any signs of modification before proceeding with the certification. If the document appears to have been altered in any way, the notary should refuse to perform the copy certification. If the notary is unsure whether the document is genuine or has been tampered with, it is always better to err on the side of caution and decline to perform the certification.

Additionally, while a notary is authorized to certify copies in California, they are not permitted to perform certification in certain circumstances when doing so may cause harm or confusion. For example, certifying a copy of a legal document such as a will could be problematic if the notary is unsure of the document's authenticity or content. In such cases, it is advisable for the notary to direct the individual to seek the assistance of an attorney or the relevant agency that can provide more thorough verification.

It is also important for notaries to be aware that the rules surrounding copy certifications may vary in other states or jurisdictions. Notaries should familiarize themselves with the specific requirements of the jurisdiction where the document will be used, especially if the document is intended for use in a foreign country. Not all notaries may be authorized to certify copies in the same way, and it is important to ensure that the certification complies with the regulations of the destination jurisdiction.

By understanding the guidelines and limitations surrounding copy certifications, notaries in California can perform their duties with confidence and integrity. They must remain vigilant in following the strict rules that govern copy certification and ensure that they never overstep their bounds. A notary's role is to verify the authenticity of a copy, not to verify the content, legality, or validity of the original document. Following these protocols will not only ensure the accuracy and legality of the notarial act but also protect the notary from potential legal consequences. With attention to detail and adherence to the rules, notaries can provide valuable services to the public and contribute to the integrity of the notarial process.

## HANDLING SIGNATURE BY MARK AND SUBSCRIBING WITNESSES

As a notary public in California, you may encounter situations where individuals cannot sign their name in the traditional manner, either due to physical limitations or illiteracy. In such cases, it is important for you as a notary to understand how to properly handle *signature by mark* and *subscribing witnesses*. Both of these scenarios are allowed under California law, but they come with specific procedures and responsibilities that must be carefully followed.

The *signature by mark* process is intended for individuals who cannot physically write their name or are unable to provide a signature for reasons such as physical disabilities or inability to write in the English language. In these situations, the person being notarized can make their mark instead of signing their name in the usual way. This mark can be any symbol, such as an "X" or any other form that the signer can make as an indication of their intent. As a notary public, you will play a crucial role in ensuring that this process is conducted in accordance with the law, safeguarding both the integrity of the notarial act and the rights of the signer.

It is essential to recognize that when a person signs by mark, the notary must be vigilant in ensuring the person understands the nature of the document being signed. This requires the notary to confirm that the signer is aware of the document's contents, just as they would in any other situation involving a standard signature. The notary must also be certain that the individual is making the mark of their own free will and is not being coerced or influenced by another party. For example, if a person who is illiterate is making an "X" on a document, you must ensure that they understand what that "X" signifies and that they willingly made it as a representation of their consent to the document's contents. This is an important part of your notarial duties, as the notary must maintain impartiality and avoid being involved in the contents of the document.

Additionally, when a signature is made by mark, the notary is required to witness the signing in person. You must be physically present during the act of signing and must not rely on a previous signature or mark. The signer's mark should be made directly on the document in the presence of the notary, ensuring that the process is fully legitimate and not subject to manipulation. You will need to ensure that the signature by mark is properly documented in your notarial journal, which is an essential record of your notarial acts. The journal entry should clearly indicate that the signer made their mark and should include any additional relevant details, such as the identity of the signer and the date and location of the notarization. This journal entry serves as a key piece of evidence in case the authenticity of the notarization is ever questioned.

For some individuals, making a mark instead of signing a document is not the only option available to them. *Subscribing witnesses* may also be involved in the notarization process when the signer is unable to personally sign the document or make a mark. A subscribing witness is a person who personally knows the signer and can confirm that the signer is the person who intended to sign the document. The subscribing witness is essentially an additional witness to the act of signing, stepping in when the signer cannot sign for themselves due to various reasons. This method is often employed in situations where the signer may be incapacitated, either temporarily or permanently, or if they are unable to sign due to physical limitations.

In California, a subscribing witness must meet certain requirements in order to fulfill their role in the notarial process. For one, the subscribing witness must be a credible person who can attest to the identity of the signer and confirm that the signer intended to sign the document. It is also important to note that the subscribing witness must be present at the time the notarial act takes place. This means that the subscribing witness must be in the same room as the notary and the signer during the notarization. The subscribing witness does not sign the document on behalf of the signer, but instead, their role is to verify that the signer's intent is properly represented and that the notary can proceed with the notarization.

When handling a notarization involving a subscribing witness, it is important to follow specific steps. First, the subscribing witness must take an oath or affirmation administered by the notary, just as the signer would. The subscribing witness's oath confirms that they are acting as a witness to the signer's intent and that they are not providing false information. You, as the notary, must ensure that the subscribing witness understands their role in the process and that they are truthful in their testimony. If the subscribing witness is unable to provide a satisfactory oath or affirmation, you should not proceed with the notarization.

Once the subscribing witness has been sworn in, they can then sign the document to affirm their role. Their signature will be recorded by the notary in the notarial journal, and the notary should make sure to include all necessary details about the subscribing witness's identity, including their name, address, and any other relevant information. The subscribing witness must also be aware that their testimony and signature are part of a legal process, and they may be held accountable if their statements are false or misleading. Therefore, the subscribing witness should act in good faith and should never provide false information in an effort to help a signer whose intent is unclear or whose identity is uncertain.

Notaries should be cautious when acting as a notary for documents involving signature by mark or subscribing witnesses. These situations can sometimes be complicated and fraught with legal and ethical considerations. For example, it is possible that a signer who wishes to make their mark may be coerced into doing so, and a subscribing witness may be pressured into providing false testimony. As a notary, it is your duty to ensure that these acts are not only done properly but also done voluntarily and in good faith.

To avoid potential pitfalls in handling these situations, notaries should always take extra care in verifying the identity of all parties involved. When a subscribing witness is present, make sure they are thoroughly vetted and confirm their relationship to the signer. The subscribing witness should be someone who can provide credible testimony about the signer's intent and identity, such as a close relative or a trustworthy acquaintance. The notary should not rely solely on the witness's word; instead, the notary should use their professional judgment to ensure that everything is in order before proceeding with the notarization.

In addition, you must remain impartial throughout the process and avoid being involved in any way with the content of the document itself. Your role is strictly to verify that the person signing the document, whether by mark or through the assistance of a subscribing witness, is doing so of their own free will and with a clear understanding of the document's contents. If at any point you believe that the signer is being coerced or is not fully aware of what they are signing, you should refuse to perform the notarization. Your primary responsibility as a notary is to ensure the integrity of the process, and that includes protecting individuals from being taken advantage of or coerced into signing a document under duress.

Handling signature by mark and subscribing witnesses may seem complex, but it is an essential part of a notary's duties in California. By thoroughly understanding the procedures, responsibilities, and limitations of these notarial acts, you will be well-equipped to carry out your duties with professionalism, integrity, and confidence. When approached with these unique situations, always be sure to adhere strictly to the law, exercise caution, and maintain the highest standards of ethical practice to safeguard the notarial process and the individuals involved.

# CHAPTER 4
## NOTARY TOOLS AND RECORD-KEEPING

### ESSENTIAL NOTARY SUPPLIES

As a notary public in California, your role is pivotal in ensuring the authenticity and legality of a wide range of documents. To carry out your duties effectively and responsibly, it is essential that you have the proper notary supplies. These supplies are the tools that empower you to perform notarizations correctly and in compliance with California law. The key supplies you will need as a notary include *seals, journals*, and *certificates*. Each of these tools plays a unique role in your responsibilities and is essential for carrying out your duties professionally. Let's dive into the specifics of each of these supplies to ensure you have a complete understanding of how they should be used and maintained.

**Seals**

The *notary seal* is perhaps the most important tool in your notary kit. It serves as a visual representation of the authority granted to you by the state of California and is used to authenticate your notarial acts. The seal must be used for every notarization you perform, and it must meet specific state requirements to be considered valid.

Under California law, your notary seal must include the following components:

1. The words *"Notary Public"*,
2. The words *"State of California"*,
3. Your name as it appears on your notary commission,
4. The words *"Commission Number"* and your commission number,
5. The words *"Commission Expiration Date"* and your commission expiration date, and
6. The county where your oath of office was filed.

The *seal* can be either a rubber stamp or an embosser, but it must be legible and durable enough to remain clear and visible on the document for years to come. The seal should also be affixed in a manner that does not obscure any part of the document's text, including signatures, dates, or other critical information.

In California, the notary seal must also be *ink-based* for most notarizations. While an embosser (which creates a raised impression) is permissible, it is not typically used for most notarial acts, as it is less practical and can sometimes be difficult to decipher. For this reason, most notaries opt for a rubber stamp that creates a clean and legible imprint. Be sure to keep your seal in good condition, replacing it as needed when the imprint begins to fade or wear down.

California law requires that your notary seal be kept in a secure location to prevent its unauthorized use. This is because the seal carries your official authority and could be used for fraudulent purposes if it falls into the wrong hands. To protect the integrity of your seal, it is best to store it in a locked drawer, a safe, or some other secure place when it is not in use.

It is important to note that the notary seal should never be used to notarize a document that has not been signed in your presence. You should never sign or seal a document before witnessing the signer's signature, and your seal should only be used to authenticate a document in conjunction with the other notarial steps.

**Journals**

The notary *journal* is another vital tool that you must use during every notarization. The journal serves as an official record of all notarial acts performed, and it provides an important safeguard in case your actions as a notary are ever questioned. California law mandates that notaries maintain a journal for the full term of their commission and for at least *seven years* after their commission expires.

Your journal should be bound and paginated, meaning each page should have a unique number to prevent any pages from being removed or altered. The journal should not have any blank spaces or gaps in between entries, as this could raise questions about the accuracy or integrity of your records. The entries must be made in chronological order, with each notarization recorded in a new, numbered entry.

Each entry in your journal should include the following details:

- *The date and time* of the notarization.
- *The type of notarization* being performed (e.g., acknowledgment, jurat, oath).
- *The full name* and *signature* of the person(s) whose document you are notarizing.
- *The type of identification* presented by the signer (e.g., driver's license, passport).
- *The signature* of any subscribing witness, if applicable.
- *A brief description* of the document being notarized (you are not required to include the entire document's contents, but a description of the document's nature is necessary).
- *The fee* charged for the notarization (if applicable).
- *Any other relevant notes* (e.g., if the signer was unable to sign by hand and made their mark, if a subscribing witness was involved, or if there were any unusual circumstances surrounding the notarization).

It is crucial that you record every notarization in your journal, even if it is a simple document. Not keeping a journal is a violation of California law, and failure to maintain accurate records could expose you to legal and financial risks. The journal not only helps protect you but also protects the public by providing a clear record of the notarial acts you've performed.

While the notary journal is a public record, it is important to understand that California law provides privacy protections for the signer. You should not disclose the contents of your journal to anyone without a valid legal reason, such as a subpoena or court order. For this reason, it is essential to keep your journal in a secure location and ensure that it is protected from unauthorized access.

In recent years, California has allowed the use of *electronic journals* for notaries who perform electronic notarizations. If you are considering using an electronic journal, ensure that it meets the state's requirements and that it is equally secure as a physical journal.

**Certificates**

Certificates are another essential component of your notary supplies. When you notarize a document, you will often be required to complete a *notarial certificate*, which is a statement that confirms that the notarization has taken place in accordance with the law. A notarial certificate will vary depending on the type of notarization being performed, such as an acknowledgment, jurat, or oath.

In California, the notarial certificate must be attached to the document being notarized. It is important that the certificate is not altered, added to, or omitted in any way that would affect the validity of the notarization.

A notarial certificate must contain the following information:

- *The name of the signer* and, in some cases, the name of a subscribing witness.
- *A statement of the notarial act* (e.g., "Subscribed and sworn to before me...," "Acknowledged before me...").
- *The date* of the notarization.
- *The notary's signature* and the *notary's seal* (the seal must be affixed directly onto the document with your signature).
- *The notary's commission information*, including the expiration date of your commission.

When completing a notarial certificate, be sure to double-check all of the details before affixing your signature and seal. If you are completing a certificate for an acknowledgment, ensure that the signer is identified properly and that the correct language is used. For a jurat, you must confirm that the signer swears or affirms the truthfulness of the document's contents in your presence.

California law requires that the notary certificate be completed with utmost accuracy. If you fail to complete a certificate correctly or leave out any required information, the notarization may be considered invalid. Additionally, the document may be rejected by the recipient, leading to frustration for both the signer and you.

As a notary public in California, your responsibility is not only to perform your duties with integrity but also to ensure that you have the proper tools and supplies to carry out those duties in accordance with the law. The notary seal, journal, and certificates are the essential supplies you need to perform notarizations effectively. Each of these supplies plays a critical role in maintaining the authenticity and legality of the notarial process. By ensuring that your supplies are up to date, properly maintained, and used correctly, you will be able to uphold the high standards of professionalism and accuracy required by California law. Always be mindful of the rules and guidelines surrounding these tools, and never hesitate to seek advice or clarification if you are ever in doubt. With the right notary supplies and a clear understanding of your responsibilities, you will be well-equipped to serve the public and carry out your duties as a notary public with confidence and competence.

## PROPER USE AND SECURITY OF THE NOTARY SEAL

As a notary public in California, the use of your notary seal is one of the most critical responsibilities entrusted to you. It is an essential tool in your notarial duties, carrying with it the legal weight of authentication for documents. Because the seal serves as a symbol of your authority and credibility as a notary public, it is of utmost importance that it is used properly and kept secure at all times. Failing to do so could result in legal consequences for both you and the parties involved in any notarized documents.

### The Notary Seal

In California, your notary seal is not just a tool to affix to documents; it is a mark of your official capacity as a notary public. The seal serves as a certification that you have properly witnessed a document and verified the identity of the signer. As part of the state's system of checks and balances, the seal helps to prevent fraudulent activities, as it provides a visual verification of the legitimacy of a document. Therefore, understanding the proper use and security of the notary seal is crucial to upholding the trust placed in you by the public and the state.

When you apply your notary seal to a document, you are affirming that the signer personally appeared before you, provided satisfactory evidence of their identity, and acknowledged their signature on the document. The notary seal's presence indicates that you, as a notary, have performed all the necessary duties required by law to verify the authenticity of the document and the identity of the signer.

The proper use of the notary seal is a clear, unambiguous process that must be followed with great attention to detail. California law specifies the components required for a valid notary seal. Your seal must include certain information: the words "*Notary Public*," the words "*State of California*," your name as it appears on your notary commission, the commission number, and the commission expiration date. It must also include the county where your oath of office was filed. These specific details ensure that the seal is linked directly to you, the notary, and that it accurately reflects your legal authority.

### How to Use the Notary Seal Properly

Properly applying the notary seal is an essential part of the notarization process. In California, the notary seal must be applied with care, and you should be familiar with the rules surrounding its use to avoid any potential issues. You are required to affix the notary seal directly on the document, alongside your signature and the notarial certificate. When applying your seal, you must ensure that it is clear, legible, and properly placed.

First, before applying your seal, ensure that you are completing a valid notarization. The signer must personally appear before you and sign the document in your presence. This is one of the first rules of notarial law: you may never apply your notary seal to a document unless you have personally witnessed the signing or have administered an oath or affirmation. If you apply your seal to a document without performing these duties, you may face serious legal consequences, including revocation of your notary commission.

Once you've witnessed the signing and confirmed that the signer is who they say they are, you will need to complete the notarial certificate. The notarial certificate includes information such as the type of notarization being performed (acknowledgment, jurat, or oath), the date, the signature of the person being notarized, and the signature of the notary (you). After completing the notarial certificate, you can then proceed to affix your notary seal.

When placing the seal, be sure that it does not obscure any of the text on the document, especially signatures, dates, or other critical information. The notary seal must not cover any important content, as this could invalidate the notarization. Ideally, you should place the seal in the notarial certificate area, which is often located at the bottom of the document. If there is not a designated space for the seal, choose an area that does not obstruct the text and ensures the seal is easily visible.

It is important to note that your notary seal must be used in conjunction with your notary signature. In California, the law requires both your signature and your seal to appear together on every notarized document. Your signature serves as a personal attestation that the notarial duties have been completed, and the seal validates your authority. If either is missing, the notarization may be considered incomplete or invalid.

**Securing the Notary Seal**

Given the significance of the notary seal, its security is paramount. If a notary's seal were to fall into the wrong hands, it could be used to create fraudulent notarizations that could harm both the notary and the public. California law places strict requirements on how notary seals should be stored and secured to prevent such misuse.

It is essential that you take steps to ensure your notary seal is always protected. One of the most important aspects of securing your seal is proper storage. California law mandates that the notary seal be kept in a *secure location*, and it is recommended that it be stored in a locked drawer, cabinet, or safe when not in use. Never leave your seal unattended or in an area where others may have access to it, as this could lead to unauthorized use.

In addition to physical security, you should also be mindful of the digital security of any notary seals that are electronically stored or used. If you use an electronic notary seal, ensure that it is protected by secure passwords, encryption, and other security measures to prevent unauthorized access. Electronic notarizations must follow the same security protocols as traditional paper notarizations to prevent fraud.

Another important security measure is ensuring that your notary seal is properly engraved or stamped. A high-quality seal will help prevent tampering, as any alteration to a stamped or embossed seal can easily be detected. If your seal begins to fade or lose its clarity, it is crucial that you replace it immediately. A worn-out seal is a security risk and can lead to challenges regarding the validity of your notarizations.

California law also requires that a notary seal be *replaced* if it is lost, stolen, or damaged. If your seal is ever lost or stolen, you must report it to the California Secretary of State immediately. Once reported, you will need to request a replacement seal and undergo the necessary steps to prevent fraudulent use of the seal. If your seal is damaged or becomes illegible, it is your responsibility to replace it at your own expense.

**Potential Consequences of Misuse**

Misusing your notary seal, whether intentionally or unintentionally, can have serious legal consequences. If your seal is used fraudulently or if it is not properly affixed to a document, you may face criminal charges, civil liability, or disciplinary action from the California Secretary of State. The use of a notary seal in a way that is not in compliance with the law could result in the revocation of your notary commission and, in severe cases, legal actions such as lawsuits or fines.

One common consequence of misuse is being accused of *"notary misconduct,"* which could be brought to light if your seal is used to notarize fraudulent or false documents. For example, if you notarize a document where the signer was not present or if you improperly alter the notarial certificate, you could be held liable for misconduct. In some cases, you could also face accusations of participating in identity theft, which could result in criminal charges.

To avoid these risks, it is essential that you adhere to all the rules and regulations surrounding the use of your notary seal. Never use the seal for documents that you have not personally witnessed, and always ensure that you are following the correct notarial procedures. By doing so, you will protect not only yourself but also the people who rely on your notarial services.

The notary seal is one of the most important tools in your notarial practice, and it must be treated with the utmost care and security. By following the appropriate steps for using and safeguarding your notary seal, you are not only complying with California law but also maintaining the trust of the public and ensuring the integrity of the notarial process. Remember that your notary seal is more than just a tool; it is a symbol of your authority and a guarantee of the legality of the documents you notarize. Always use it with precision, security, and attention to detail. Your diligence will help you uphold the professionalism and reliability expected of a notary public in California.

## MAINTAINING A COMPLIANT NOTARY JOURNAL

Maintaining a compliant notary journal is one of the most essential duties a notary public in California must fulfill. A notary journal is not just a book where you jot down notes; it is a vital record that serves as proof of your notarial acts. California law requires that notaries keep a detailed journal of each notarial act they perform. This notary journal acts as both a safeguard for you and a critical element in ensuring the integrity of the notarization process. It helps prevent fraud, protects your legal rights as a notary, and provides a clear record of your activities should a question arise about any of your notarizations.

As a notary public, you have a legal obligation to maintain this journal. In California, the law is clear: *you must keep a notary journal for all notarial acts performed*, with very few exceptions. Failure to maintain a compliant notary journal could result in legal penalties, including fines and the loss of your notary commission. Therefore, understanding what is required of you when maintaining this journal is crucial for both your professional success and the protection of all parties involved in the notarization process.

**Understanding the Role of the Notary Journal**

The notary journal serves as an official record of all notarial acts you perform. Its primary purpose is to ensure that there is an accurate, written account of each transaction, providing transparency and accountability. For instance, if a dispute arises regarding a notarized document, the journal acts as evidence that you followed proper procedures. Should your notarial act be questioned in a court of law, your journal could be used to verify that you properly identified the signer and that all legal requirements were met.

By keeping a comprehensive notary journal, you create a defense for yourself against allegations of misconduct or improper notarization. If someone challenges the validity of a document you notarized, your journal serves as your defense, showing that you adhered to the law and followed all necessary steps to ensure a proper notarization. This is why maintaining a detailed, accurate, and compliant journal is critical to your professional reputation as a notary.

**Requirements for Notary Journal Entries in California**

California law is very specific about the types of information that must be included in your notary journal. These entries must be made in chronological order, and each entry should be clear, legible, and easily understandable. The following are the mandatory components that must be included for every notarial act you perform:

First, you must record the *date* and *time* of each notarial act. This helps establish a timeline of events and is important for verifying when a particular notarization took place. Each entry should include the complete date (month, day, year), along with the exact time of the notarization.

Next, the journal must include the *type of notarization performed*. In California, notaries can perform various types of notarizations, such as acknowledgments, jurats, oaths, and affirmations. For each entry, you must clearly indicate what type of notarial act you performed. This helps distinguish between different types of documents and serves as a useful reference in case of future inquiries.

You are also required to record the *name of each signer*. You must write down the full name of the individual whose signature you are notarizing. This ensures that there is a direct record of who signed the document. Additionally, you must indicate whether you personally identified the signer or whether the signer was known to you, as well as the type of identification used (such as a driver's license or passport) if you relied on a document for identification purposes. The law requires that you document the *type of identification* presented by the signer.

Another crucial element that must be recorded is the *signature of the person whose signature was notarized*. This acts as a record of the person's agreement to be notarized, and it serves as a clear identifier that the signer was involved in the notarization process.

For documents that are being notarized, you must note the *title of the document* being signed. It is important to accurately record this information because it clarifies what specific document you were notarizing. This protects you from any future claims that the notarization was related to a different document than the one you actually witnessed.

Additionally, your journal must include a *thumbprint* of the signer if you are notarizing a deed, quitclaim deed, deed of trust, or any document affecting real property. California law requires that a thumbprint be placed in the journal for these specific documents, as it adds an extra layer of security and verification to the notarization process.

Finally, you must also document whether the notarization was done with a *fee* or not, indicating how much you charged for the notarial service. The law requires that you note this information in your journal, which helps keep track of your earnings and ensures that your business practices remain transparent.

**Journal Entries: Best Practices**

While California law provides a clear framework for what must be included in each journal entry, the way in which you maintain your journal is just as important. Keeping your journal entries organized, accurate, and consistent is essential to maintaining compliance with California law and ensuring the validity of your notarial acts.

One of the best practices when maintaining a notary journal is to make your entries *immediately* after performing the notarization. It is important that you do not delay or wait until later to make entries, as doing so could result in incomplete or inaccurate records. If you wait too long to make an entry, you may forget key details, and your journal may not reflect the true nature of the notarization.

It is also essential that all entries be made in *permanent ink*—a pencil or erasable pen should never be used. If an error is made, it should be crossed out with a single line, and the correct information should be written above it. This ensures that the journal remains a permanent and accurate record, which can be critical in any legal dispute.

# California Notary Handbook 2025

As a notary, you must be aware of the importance of protecting the confidentiality of the information in your journal. The contents of your journal are private and should only be accessed by authorized individuals, such as law enforcement or the California Secretary of State, in the event of an investigation or audit. You should never allow others to inspect your journal unless required by law, and you should store your journal securely when not in use. Many notaries store their journals in locked cabinets, safes, or other secure locations to prevent unauthorized access.

## How to Handle Journal Security

Because your notary journal contains sensitive personal information, it is your responsibility to ensure that it is securely stored at all times. California law requires that you keep your notary journal *in a secure location* to prevent unauthorized access or potential tampering. This includes keeping the journal in a locked drawer, safe, or cabinet when not in use. Failure to maintain the security of your journal could result in penalties or the revocation of your notary commission.

If your journal is lost or stolen, you must report the incident to the California Secretary of State immediately. Additionally, you may need to notify any individuals whose information was contained in the journal to help protect their identity. In some cases, you may be required to provide a copy of the journal entries that were compromised, especially if they were related to a specific notarization involving real property.

California law mandates that you keep your journal for *at least five years* after the last entry. Even after your commission expires, you must retain your journal for this period. If you cease to be a notary, you are responsible for ensuring that your journal is securely stored and accessible if needed. If you retire from notary work or move out of state, you should contact the California Secretary of State to determine the appropriate procedure for handling your journal.

## When You May Be Asked to Provide Your Journal

Your notary journal could be requested for inspection under several circumstances. For example, the California Secretary of State may conduct periodic audits of notaries to ensure that they are complying with state regulations. In such cases, you must make your journal available for review and provide any requested information.

Law enforcement agencies or other authorized individuals may also request to inspect your journal if there is a legal investigation or case involving notarized documents. If you are subpoenaed to produce your journal, you must comply with the request, provided it is legally authorized.

Maintaining a compliant notary journal is one of your most important responsibilities as a notary public in California. It ensures that you are following the law and maintaining transparency, security, and accuracy in your notarial acts. By recording all required information in your journal, keeping it secure, and following best practices, you can protect both your notarial practice and the individuals who rely on your services. Adhering to these regulations will also help you avoid any legal consequences and ensure that your notary career remains successful and reputable.

## RECORD RETENTION POLICIES AND BEST PRACTICES

Record retention policies are a crucial component of a notary public's responsibilities in California. As a notary, you are required to maintain thorough and accurate records of the notarizations you perform. These records serve not only as a safeguard for you, the notary, but also as protection for the individuals and organizations relying on your services. California law is clear about the necessity of record retention and the specific requirements governing the retention of notarial records, including your journal, certificates, and other supporting documentation.

The process of retaining records is not just about fulfilling a legal obligation; it is about ensuring that the integrity and validity of your work are protected over time. The primary role of proper record retention is to provide a reliable and verifiable history of your notarial acts. If any questions arise about your notarizations, whether it's due to a dispute, a legal challenge, or an investigation, your records act as the evidence that can verify your actions and provide clarity.

When you take on the responsibility of a notary public, you are entering a professional role that requires you to keep accurate, detailed, and secure records. This chapter will guide you through the best practices and legal obligations for maintaining proper record retention, ensuring your compliance with California laws, and safeguarding the integrity of your notarial work.

**Legal Requirements for Record Retention in California**

California law outlines specific rules that notaries must follow regarding record retention. One of the primary legal requirements for notaries in California is that they must retain their notary journal for at least *five years* after the date of the last notarization recorded in the journal. This is a mandatory retention period established under California Government Code Section 8206. This retention period ensures that you have a complete record of your notarial acts available should any questions arise.

It is essential to understand that even if your notary commission expires or is revoked, you are still required to retain your journal for the full *five-year* period. In other words, the duty to retain records does not end simply because you are no longer a notary. Similarly, if you decide to cease being a notary or move out of state, you must still adhere to this retention period. This can be challenging for some, but it is necessary to ensure that you comply with the law and maintain the integrity of your notarial activities.

Furthermore, if you lose your notary journal or if it is stolen, California law mandates that you report the loss to the *California Secretary of State* immediately. This is a crucial step to protect the security of the information in your journal. If the journal is lost or stolen, you should also notify your clients and the parties whose information may have been compromised. It is vital to take swift action in these situations to minimize potential risks.

Along with your journal, you are also required to retain *copies of all notarial certificates* you issue. While California law does not mandate a specific length of time for retaining certificates, it is considered good practice to keep copies for at least the same *five-year* period. Notary certificates are part of your official records and may be referenced if the notarized documents are ever called into question. These certificates are critical pieces of evidence that demonstrate you have followed the legal process in performing a notarization.

**Best Practices for Maintaining a Notary Journal**

The notary journal is your most important record-keeping tool, and it is crucial that you maintain it with the highest level of care. Not only does California law require you to keep a journal, but the way in which you maintain and safeguard that journal is just as important. Let's take a closer look at the best practices for maintaining a compliant notary journal.

First, it is vital that you record all the necessary information required by California law for each notarization. This includes the *date* and *time* of the notarization, the *type of notarial act* performed, the *name of the signer*, the *type of identification* presented, and any other relevant details. Every entry should be made promptly and legibly to avoid confusion and ensure the information is accurate. If you make an error, it should be crossed out with a single line, and the correct information should be written above it. Avoid using pencil or erasable ink for making entries in your journal.

Second, you should record the details in *chronological order*. This ensures that your journal is organized and easy to reference. You should make entries immediately after performing each notarization, rather than waiting until later, as this reduces the chances of missing important details or making mistakes.

Another best practice is to *protect the security* of your journal. Your journal contains sensitive personal information, and it must be stored in a secure location when not in use. Locking the journal in a drawer, safe, or other secure storage area is an excellent way to safeguard it from unauthorized access. If you work from home or in a mobile setting, you should ensure that your journal is never left unattended or in an unsecured location.

Additionally, you should take care to only allow authorized individuals to inspect your journal. You must comply with any legal requests from the *California Secretary of State* or law enforcement, but otherwise, your journal should remain private. It is important to understand that unauthorized inspection of your journal could violate your clients' privacy rights and potentially expose you to legal liability.

**Storing and Securing Electronic Notary Records**

In today's digital age, many notaries are beginning to use electronic journals and digital notary tools. Electronic notary journals provide the same functionality as physical paper journals but with the added benefit of digital storage and ease of access. However, even when maintaining electronic records, notaries must comply with the same legal requirements for record retention.

If you choose to use an electronic journal, it is essential to ensure that the platform you use complies with California's notary laws. The electronic journal must allow you to capture all of the same details that are required in a paper journal, including the date and time, the type of notarization, the name of the signer, and identification details. Additionally, the system should include security measures to protect the data, such as encryption and password protection.

If your journal is electronic, you must still retain a *backup copy* of the journal to ensure that you do not lose valuable records due to a system failure or technical issue. It is recommended that you back up your journal regularly to an external hard drive or secure cloud storage service. This ensures that your records are safe and accessible even if your primary system experiences issues.

As with paper journals, electronic notary journals must be stored securely, and unauthorized individuals should not have access to them. This includes ensuring that your computer or device is protected with strong passwords, biometric security features, or other safeguards. If you store your journal on a cloud-based platform, make sure that the service complies with California's data security regulations.

**Destroying Notary Records**

At the end of the mandatory retention period, after the *five-year* holding period has expired, you may decide to destroy your notary journal or certificates. However, before you destroy any notarial records, you must ensure that it is done in a manner that prevents unauthorized access to the information. Simply throwing away your journal or certificates in the trash is not an acceptable method of disposal.

The best practice for destroying notary records is to use a *shredder* capable of destroying paper records beyond recognition. If you are storing records electronically, you should delete them in a manner that ensures they cannot be recovered or accessed by others. For electronic records, this means using proper data deletion tools that meet industry standards for secure disposal.

Before destroying any records, it is also recommended that you keep a *final record* of the destruction, noting the date and method of disposal. This can help you maintain accountability and provide evidence that you properly disposed of your records when required.

**Special Considerations for Real Property Documents**

Certain documents, such as deeds and powers of attorney, may require special attention when it comes to record retention. For example, *California law mandates that a notary must retain a thumbprint* in the journal for any notarization involving the transfer of real property (such as deeds and quitclaim deeds). This thumbprint serves as an additional layer of verification for these high-risk transactions and helps prevent fraud.

As with other notarial records, these journal entries, including the thumbprints, must be kept for the required *five years*. It is important to understand that, in these cases, the retention period may extend beyond the period for other types of notarizations. Additionally, should these records be requested by law enforcement or other authorities, it is crucial that you provide them promptly and fully.

**Managing Records After the End of Your Commission**

When your notary commission expires or is revoked, you must follow the proper procedure for handling your records. California law requires you to *turn over your records* to the *California Secretary of State* if your commission expires or if you cease to be a notary public. This ensures that your records are maintained in a secure location, and it prevents the misuse of your journal or certificates.

If you are moving out of state or retiring from notarial work, it is important to take the necessary steps to transfer your records in accordance with California law. If you cannot transfer them to the state, you are responsible for ensuring that the records are kept secure and accessible if needed for future inquiries.

Record retention is a fundamental responsibility for all notaries public in California. By understanding and adhering to the legal requirements and best practices outlined above, you can ensure that your notarial records are maintained in a compliant and secure manner. The integrity of your notarial acts depends on your commitment to accurate and thorough recordkeeping. Whether you are handling traditional paper records or utilizing electronic tools, you must ensure that your records are protected and accessible, offering transparency and security for all parties involved. By maintaining proper records, you protect not only your own professional reputation but also the trust that others place in your notarial services.

California Notary Handbook 2025

# CHAPTER 5
## IDENTIFYING SIGNERS AND PREVENTING FRAUD

### ACCEPTABLE FORMS OF IDENTIFICATION IN CALIFORNIA

When you take on the responsibilities of a notary public in California, one of the most crucial aspects of your work involves verifying the identity of the individuals you are assisting. A notary's primary duty is to ensure that the person requesting the notarization is indeed who they claim to be. To fulfill this responsibility accurately, a notary must rely on specific forms of identification to confirm a signer's identity. Knowing what identification is acceptable, as well as how to assess it, is paramount in ensuring that notarizations are legitimate, secure, and compliant with California law.

In California, the rules surrounding acceptable forms of identification are set forth by the state's notary laws, particularly the California Government Code and the California Code of Regulations. Understanding the range of identification types that you can accept, as well as the criteria for their use, is vital to your role as a notary. This chapter will walk you through the identification requirements for notaries, outlining what forms are permissible, how to verify their authenticity, and how to handle situations where acceptable identification is not provided.

**The Basics of Acceptable Identification**

As a notary public, your primary job is to ensure that the person requesting notarization is the person they claim to be. To do this, you must verify their identity through a reliable, government-issued identification document. Acceptable forms of identification must contain specific information to be considered valid. In California, the identification used for notarial purposes must meet a few key requirements. These include providing a photo, the name of the person, and other specific identifying details such as a physical description, date of birth, and an expiration date. The most commonly used form of identification for notarizations is a government-issued photo ID, such as a driver's license or passport.

However, not all forms of identification are universally acceptable. Some identification documents do not meet the necessary criteria for confirming identity in the notarial context. Understanding which documents you can accept—and how to ensure that they meet legal standards—is one of the most critical tasks you will face as a notary.

**Acceptable Forms of Identification**

The most common forms of acceptable identification in California for notarial acts are as follows:

1. **California Driver's License or Identification Card**: A valid California driver's license or ID card is widely recognized as a standard form of identification. It provides a clear photograph of the individual, their full

legal name, and other essential details, such as their address, date of birth, and signature. The card must be current—meaning that the expiration date should not have passed. If the document is expired, it is generally not acceptable unless the individual can provide additional proof of identity.

2. **United States Passport**: A U.S. passport, whether for travel or as an identification card, is another form of identification you can accept. A passport contains detailed information about the individual, including their photograph, full name, date of birth, and nationality. Similar to the driver's license, the passport should be current, and it should not be expired for more than a year to be acceptable.

3. **Foreign Passport**: In some cases, a foreign passport can be used as identification for a notarization, provided it meets the necessary requirements for identification. A foreign passport must include a photograph and be issued by the government of a foreign country. It should also be valid (not expired) and contain enough identifying details to confirm the individual's identity.

4. **California Identification Card for Minors**: California issues identification cards for minors, which are also acceptable forms of identification for notarization purposes. These cards must contain the minor's full name, photograph, signature, and other necessary identifying details. While not as commonly used as adult identification, it is still recognized by California law.

5. **Military Identification Card**: A U.S. military identification card is a valid form of identification for notarizations. These cards include a photograph of the individual, their full name, rank, and other identifying information. As with all identification documents, the military ID must be current and not expired for more than a year.

**Identification by Credible Witnesses**

In some situations, the person seeking notarization may not have an acceptable form of identification. In these cases, California law allows the use of a *credible witness* to verify the identity of the signer. A *credible witness* is someone who personally knows the signer and is willing to swear under oath that the signer is who they say they are.

For a credible witness to be acceptable, they must meet a few criteria. The first requirement is that the witness must know the signer personally, meaning they must have a relationship that goes beyond just meeting the individual at the time of the notarization. Additionally, the credible witness must be able to present their own valid form of identification. The credible witness cannot be a party to the transaction being notarized, and they must be able to swear that the signer is the person they claim to be. In cases where credible witnesses are used, the notary must record the name and address of the witness in the notary journal, along with their signature and other pertinent details.

# California Notary Handbook 2025

## Verifying Identification

Simply accepting a form of identification is not enough. As a notary, it is your responsibility to verify that the identification presented to you is valid, unexpired, and not altered in any way. This means checking for key details such as the following:

- **Photograph**: Ensure that the photograph on the identification matches the person presenting it. This is one of the most basic yet effective ways of verifying identity.
- **Expiration Date**: Check that the expiration date on the ID has not passed. An expired ID is generally not acceptable, unless the person can prove their identity with additional supporting documents.
- **Physical Description**: Many forms of identification, such as driver's licenses, contain a physical description of the individual, such as height, weight, and eye color. Compare these details with the person standing before you.
- **Holograms and Watermarks**: Modern IDs often have security features such as holograms, watermarks, and special ink that make them difficult to counterfeit. Be sure to examine these features closely to determine the authenticity of the ID.

In some cases, a signer may present identification that does not meet these requirements. If the identification appears to be altered or counterfeit, or if it simply does not include enough information to establish identity, it is your duty as a notary to refuse the notarization. If you are unsure about the validity of an ID, err on the side of caution and do not proceed with the notarization until the proper identification is presented.

## Handling Special Circumstances

Notaries occasionally encounter unusual situations that require careful judgment regarding identification. For example, individuals may be unable to provide a standard form of ID due to a number of reasons, such as homelessness, loss of identification, or other factors. In such cases, the notary may accept a *credible witness* as described earlier, but the rules for identifying credible witnesses must be followed carefully.

Additionally, in some circumstances, individuals may be unable to present a photo ID due to cultural or religious reasons. If this occurs, you may want to ask the signer for other forms of evidence, such as a combination of documents that confirm their identity, or ask them to provide a credible witness who can verify their identity.

## Legal Considerations and Risks

Notaries must be aware of the risks involved in accepting improper identification. Failure to verify a signer's identity correctly could lead to serious legal consequences. If a notarized document is later challenged in court or during a transaction, you could be held liable for any fraudulent activity that occurred because of your failure to properly verify the identity of the signer.

For example, if you notarize a document for an individual who presented fraudulent identification and the transaction later leads to legal action, you may be required to provide your notarial journal and testify in court. If it is found that you neglected to verify the ID properly, you could be exposed to civil or criminal penalties, and your notary commission could be revoked.

**Maintaining a Safe and Secure Notarial Practice**

As a notary, you must always take precautions to protect your clients' personal information. This means ensuring that the details of the signer's identification are kept confidential and secure. Be sure to securely store any documents related to the notarization process, and remember to follow proper procedures when filling out your notary journal.

Additionally, if you encounter any concerns about fraudulent documents or the identification of a signer, you should report these concerns to the appropriate authorities. California law provides mechanisms for reporting fraudulent activity, and you must take these steps if you suspect that a signer is using false identification or engaging in a deceptive transaction.

In your role as a notary public in California, verifying the identity of the individuals you assist is one of the most critical responsibilities you have. The forms of identification you accept must be valid, reliable, and in accordance with California law. By following the guidelines provided for acceptable identification and by carefully verifying the authenticity of every ID presented, you will ensure that your notarizations are legally sound, secure, and above reproach. Always take the time to inspect identification thoroughly and remain diligent in your efforts to protect both your clients and yourself from fraud or misrepresentation. By doing so, you will maintain the integrity and professionalism of your notarial practice.

## PROCEDURES FOR VERIFYING SIGNER IDENTITY

Verifying the identity of signers is one of the most crucial tasks a notary public faces. The integrity of the notarial process hinges on ensuring that the individual before you is, in fact, the person they claim to be. As a notary in California, your ability to properly verify a signer's identity is not only a legal obligation but also a safeguard against fraud, identity theft, and other forms of deception. This chapter will delve into the procedures for verifying signer identity, discussing various identification methods, the use of credible witnesses, and how to assess and document identity verification in compliance with California law.

**Importance of Identity Verification**

Identity verification is central to the purpose of notarization. Whether you are notarizing a deed, power of attorney, affidavit, or any other legal document, confirming the identity of the signer ensures that the transaction is legitimate and that the signer is not being coerced or acting under fraudulent pretenses. Without proper identity verification, notarization would lose its reliability and legal standing.

California notaries are required to verify the identity of individuals before performing notarial acts, such as administering an oath, taking an acknowledgment, or certifying a copy of a document. This verification is done through the presentation of *acceptable identification* and, in some cases, through *credible witnesses* who can vouch for the signer's identity. As a notary, you must follow specific procedures when verifying identity to ensure compliance with state laws and to maintain the integrity of your notarial acts.

**Acceptable Forms of Identification**

The cornerstone of identity verification is the presentation of proper identification. Under California law, a notary must ensure that the identification documents presented are current, unaltered, and issued by a government agency. The following types of identification are typically acceptable for notarization purposes:

- **California Driver's License or Identification Card**: This is the most common and widely accepted form of identification in California. It provides a clear photograph of the individual, their name, date of birth, signature, and address. The card must be current, and the expiration date should not have passed.

- **U.S. Passport**: A valid U.S. passport, whether used for travel or as a form of identification, contains key information such as the individual's name, photograph, date of birth, and nationality. The passport should be current and free from any alterations.

- **Foreign Passport**: A foreign passport may also be used if it meets certain criteria. It must be issued by the government of another country and must include a photograph, the individual's name, and other identifying details. The passport must be valid and not expired for more than a year.

- **Other Government-Issued IDs**: Military identification cards and other government-issued identification documents, such as those issued by federal, state, or tribal agencies, may also be acceptable, provided they contain a photograph and the necessary identifying details.

When a signer presents identification, you must verify that it meets these requirements. The document must be in good condition—no signs of tampering, alteration, or damage. If the ID appears suspicious, you must refuse to perform the notarization until a valid form of identification is provided.

**Verifying Identification**

Verification of identification is more than just accepting the documents at face value. As a notary, you are tasked with closely inspecting the ID to ensure its authenticity. Pay careful attention to the following elements:

- **Photograph**: The photo on the identification must clearly match the individual who is presenting the document. The notary should compare the photograph with the signer to ensure they are the same person.

- **Expiration Date**: The ID must not be expired. An expired ID is typically not acceptable unless the signer can provide other evidence to confirm their identity. For example, an expired passport might be accepted if it's accompanied by other corroborating documents.

- **Physical Description**: Many identification documents, such as driver's licenses, include a physical description of the person. The description may include height, weight, eye color, and other characteristics. Verify that these match the person standing before you.

- **Security Features**: Modern identification cards often contain security features such as holograms, watermarks, microprinting, and ultraviolet ink. These features are designed to prevent counterfeiting, and it is important that notaries familiarize themselves with them. Inspect the ID carefully for these features, especially if the document looks unusual or suspect.

- **Consistency of Information**: Ensure that the name on the ID matches the name on the document the signer is presenting. If there are discrepancies between the name on the ID and the document, you may need to ask the signer for additional documentation to confirm their identity.

**Credible Witnesses**

There may be occasions when a signer cannot present acceptable identification due to loss, theft, or other circumstances. In these cases, California law allows for the use of *credible witnesses*. A credible witness is someone who personally knows the signer and can vouch for their identity. In this scenario, the notary relies on the witness to confirm that the signer is who they claim to be.

To use a credible witness, the witness must meet certain requirements. First, the witness must be personally known to the signer. This means the witness should be someone with a relationship to the signer that goes beyond just meeting them at the time of the notarization. Additionally, the witness must present their own valid form of identification to the notary to prove their identity.

There are two types of credible witnesses in California: a *single* credible witness or *two* credible witnesses. The use of a single credible witness is generally acceptable when that individual knows both the signer and the notary. In cases where the signer cannot provide any form of identification, two credible witnesses may be required. These witnesses should each provide a valid ID and swear under oath that the signer is the individual they claim to be. In all cases, the notary must record the names and addresses of the credible witnesses in their journal, along with their signatures and other pertinent details.

It is important to note that the credible witness must not be a party to the transaction being notarized. For example, if the document being notarized is related to a financial transaction, the witness must not be involved in that transaction. Additionally, the witness cannot be a family member or someone who stands to benefit from the notarization.

### Documenting the Verification Process

As part of your notarial duties, you must record the verification of the signer's identity in your notary journal. This is a critical step that helps ensure that the notarization is legally valid and traceable. California law requires that the notary record specific details about the identification used to verify the signer's identity, including the type of ID, the document number, and the issuing agency.

For instance, if the signer presents a California driver's license, you should document the driver's license number, the state of issuance, and the expiration date in your journal. Additionally, if a credible witness is used, you must include the witness's details—such as their name, address, and the type of ID they presented. If two credible witnesses are used, both of their details must be recorded.

This record-keeping is essential not only for legal compliance but also for protecting yourself in case of future disputes or challenges to the notarization. If someone contests the notarization or alleges fraud, your journal entries can serve as proof that the identity verification process was properly followed.

### Handling Situations of Suspicion

In some cases, you may find that a signer's identification appears suspicious or that there are inconsistencies in the information they provide. If you suspect that the signer is using false identification, is attempting to commit fraud, or is under duress, you have an obligation to refuse the notarization.

For example, if the identification appears to have been altered, or if the photograph on the ID does not match the signer, you should not proceed with the notarization. Similarly, if a credible witness cannot provide sufficient proof of their own identity or if their story seems inconsistent, it is best to err on the side of caution and deny the notarization.

If you do refuse a notarization due to suspicious circumstances, you must document your decision in your notary journal. It is also a good idea to report any fraudulent activities to the appropriate authorities to prevent further issues.

Verifying the identity of the signer is an essential part of your duties as a notary public in California. The procedures for identity verification are designed to protect both the public and the integrity of the notarization process. By understanding the acceptable forms of identification, properly verifying their authenticity, and documenting the process, you ensure that your notarial acts are valid, secure, and legally sound.

As a notary, it is your responsibility to be vigilant, thorough, and conscientious when verifying identity. Whether you are dealing with a standard identification document, working with a credible witness, or handling a situation where identification is not available, always adhere to the guidelines and procedures established by California law. This will help you build trust, maintain professionalism, and safeguard against fraud or misrepresentation in your notarial practice.

## RECOGNIZING AND ADDRESSING SIGNS OF COERCION OR DURESS

As a notary public in California, one of your most important roles is to ensure that the signer is acting of their own free will when performing any notarial act. A key part of this responsibility is recognizing signs of *coercion* or *duress*, where a person may be forced or threatened into signing a document against their will. These circumstances could lead to fraudulent or invalid notarizations, and as a notary, you must take steps to prevent such situations from occurring. This chapter explores how to recognize the signs of coercion or duress and what actions to take if you suspect a signer is not acting voluntarily.

**Understanding Coercion and Duress**

Coercion and duress refer to situations where a person is pressured or forced to act against their will. This could involve physical force, threats, intimidation, manipulation, or even undue influence. The key element in both cases is the lack of free will; the individual is not making a decision or taking an action voluntarily but is instead doing so because of an external force or threat.

In the context of notarization, coercion or duress can manifest in various ways. The signer may feel threatened by another person present in the room, or they might be under duress due to a threatening situation outside of the notarial process. For example, someone may be coerced into signing a legal document by a family member, business partner, or even an authority figure. The document being notarized could be a contract, a will, a deed, or a power of attorney—any document that can be used to exert control or pressure over an individual.

**Signs of Coercion or Duress**

As a notary, it is your duty to be vigilant and aware of the signs of coercion or duress. While every situation is unique, there are common indicators you can watch for. Some of these signs are more subtle, while others may be more obvious. Here are several key red flags that might suggest a signer is under duress or being coerced:

- **Body Language**: One of the first indicators of duress is the signer's body language. If the signer appears visibly uncomfortable, anxious, or distressed while signing, it could be a sign that they are not acting voluntarily. Look for signs such as clenched fists, avoiding eye contact, shaking, or nervousness. While some people may naturally be nervous during the notarization process, it's essential to distinguish between general anxiety and the more serious signs of being under pressure.

- **Verbal Cues**: A signer under duress may exhibit verbal signs of distress, such as speaking in a hesitant or fearful manner, avoiding answering questions directly, or showing signs of reluctance when asked if they are signing voluntarily. They may even vocalize that they feel pressured or that they are only signing because they are being forced to do so. If a signer makes any such statements, it's crucial to proceed with caution.

- **Discomfort in the Presence of Another Person**: If there is a third party present who seems to be influencing or intimidating the signer, it's essential to be alert. If the signer is hesitant to speak openly in front of the other person, or if they appear to be looking to the third party for reassurance or approval before signing, these are red flags. In some cases, the third party may be actively prompting or pressuring the signer to act against their will.

- **Inconsistent Behavior or Stories**: If a signer is behaving inconsistently or contradicting themselves about the document or their situation, this could indicate that they are not freely consenting to the action. For example, if a signer seems unsure about the contents of the document or is unable to explain why they are signing it, this might be a sign of coercion. The signer may also hesitate to answer questions about the purpose or significance of the document.

- **Overly Confident or Aggressive Third Parties**: If another individual present is overly assertive or dominant during the notarization process, it can be a sign that the signer is being coerced. This could include someone who speaks for the signer, tries to control the conversation, or tries to dictate how the document should be signed. Be aware of any behavior that seeks to limit the signer's ability to make independent decisions.

- **Physical Indicators of Harm**: In extreme cases, physical signs of harm, such as bruising or other injuries, may indicate that the signer is being physically coerced or abused. If you notice any signs of physical harm or if the signer appears to be in fear of someone else present, take immediate steps to ensure their safety and wellbeing. It is vital to protect the individual from further harm, and you may need to contact authorities to intervene.

## Legal Implications of Coercion or Duress

California law is clear that a notarial act must be performed willingly and without coercion. If a signer is under duress or is coerced into signing a document, the notarial act may be invalid, and the document itself could be challenged in court. In the case of a will, for instance, if it is discovered that a person was forced or manipulated into signing the document, the will could be contested, and the signer's true wishes may not be honored.

Furthermore, if you notarize a document that you know or suspect was signed under duress, you could face legal consequences, including charges of misconduct or fraud. In the worst-case scenario, you could be held liable for any resulting harm or damage that comes from the notarization. California law holds notaries to a high standard of professional conduct, and knowingly notarizing a document under coercion or duress is not only unethical but illegal.

## What to Do If You Suspect Coercion or Duress

As a notary, it is your responsibility to ensure that the signer is acting voluntarily. If you suspect coercion or duress, you must take steps to protect both the signer and yourself. Here's what you should do if you believe a signer is not acting of their own free will:

- **Refuse to Notarize**: If you have any reasonable doubt that the signer is acting voluntarily, you are obligated to refuse to notarize the document. Even if the signer insists that they want to proceed, it is better to err on the side of caution and avoid proceeding with a notarization that could later be contested. A notarization performed under duress could lead to significant legal complications down the line.

- **Separate the Signer from the Third Party**: If a third party is present and you suspect they are exerting pressure on the signer, try to separate the signer from that individual in a private setting. Ask the signer directly whether they are signing voluntarily, and listen carefully to their response. Do not rely solely on the opinions or statements of the third party. Your job is to ensure the signer's free will, and this can only be assessed through direct communication with the signer themselves.

- **Document the Incident**: If you are unable to proceed with the notarization due to suspicion of coercion or duress, document everything in your notary journal. Record any signs of coercion or duress you observed, as well as any relevant conversations or statements made by the signer. This record can help protect you in case there are questions or legal challenges regarding the notarization.

- **Contact Authorities**: If the situation seems to involve immediate harm or if the signer is in physical danger, you must contact law enforcement authorities. You may also consider contacting other professionals, such as a lawyer or mediator, if the situation requires legal intervention. Your primary concern should always be the safety and well-being of the signer.

## Protecting Yourself as a Notary

While it is your duty to recognize signs of coercion or duress, it is also important to protect yourself in these situations. The best way to avoid liability and legal complications is to be diligent in your notarial practices and to document everything thoroughly. Keep detailed records of all notarial acts, including the circumstances surrounding each one. If you ever find yourself in a situation where you suspect coercion, do not hesitate to err on the side of caution and refuse to notarize the document until you can ensure that the signer is acting voluntarily.

Furthermore, consider providing your signers with clear instructions before the notarization takes place. Let them know that they are under no obligation to proceed if they are not comfortable with the process, and that they have the right to ask questions and seek clarification about the document being signed. This transparency can help ensure that the signer feels empowered and that they are acting with full knowledge and consent.

Recognizing and addressing signs of coercion or duress is a critical aspect of your role as a notary. By being aware of the warning signs, understanding the legal implications, and following the proper procedures, you can help ensure that your notarial acts are valid, secure, and free from the influence of coercion or duress. The trust placed in you as a notary is an important responsibility, and it is up to you to uphold the integrity of the notarization process.

## PREVENTING FRAUDULENT TRANSACTIONS AND IMPERSONATIONS

As a notary public in California, you play a critical role in safeguarding the integrity of the legal process. Notaries are often trusted with verifying the identity of individuals, authenticating signatures, and ensuring that all documents are signed voluntarily and with the appropriate understanding. Because of this responsibility, notaries must be diligent in preventing fraudulent transactions and impersonations, as these can have significant legal and financial consequences.

**Understanding the Risk of Fraudulent Transactions and Impersonations**

Fraudulent transactions and impersonations are criminal acts that often involve deception for personal or financial gain. In the context of notarial services, fraud can occur in a variety of ways. For example, individuals may attempt to present false identities or forged documents in order to carry out illegal activities such as identity theft, financial fraud, or the unauthorized transfer of property. These fraudulent actions can cause serious harm to both the individuals involved and the broader community.

Impersonation, on the other hand, involves one person pretending to be someone else in order to deceive a notary into performing an act based on false information. This could involve someone attempting to notarize a document by pretending to be the actual signer, or someone trying to trick a notary into notarizing a document for a person who is not physically present.

As a notary, your primary responsibility is to prevent such fraudulent activities by verifying the identity of the signer, ensuring the document's authenticity, and carefully observing the entire process to make sure that everything is above board.

**Key Strategies for Preventing Fraudulent Transactions**

There are several important strategies and practices that you can adopt to prevent fraudulent transactions and impersonations in your notarial work. These methods are grounded in the principles of vigilance, thoroughness, and documentation. Let's take a closer look at some of the most effective ways to safeguard yourself, your clients, and the legal integrity of your work.

**1. Verifying the Signer's Identity**

One of the most critical steps in preventing fraud is verifying the identity of the individual requesting the notarization. California law requires notaries to confirm that the person appearing before them is the individual named in the document and is signing voluntarily. This is where the proper verification of identification documents becomes essential.

Always ask the signer to provide *valid, government-issued identification* (ID) that includes their photograph and signature. Some common forms of acceptable ID in California include a driver's license, passport, or state-issued identification card. Be sure to carefully inspect the ID for any signs of tampering or discrepancies. Look for things such as altered information, expiration dates, and unusual features that might suggest the ID has been forged.

In cases where a signer does not have an acceptable form of ID, or if you have doubts about the authenticity of the identification provided, you may need to use an alternative method for identity verification. California notaries can accept credible witnesses—people who personally know the signer and can vouch for their identity. The credible witness must sign an oath before the notary and provide a valid ID themselves. This process should be done with great care to ensure that the witness is legitimate and trustworthy.

## 2. Scrutinizing the Document

Before proceeding with a notarization, it is vital to examine the document in question to ensure that it is legitimate. Be sure that the document appears to be complete, with no missing sections or blank spaces. Any document that contains areas left blank could be a red flag for potential fraud. Fraudsters may attempt to have a document notarized with blank sections, which they can later fill in with fraudulent information.

In addition to checking for blank spaces, review the document carefully to ensure that it is consistent with the person's identity and circumstances. For instance, if the document is a power of attorney, make sure that the signer's name matches the name on the ID they provided. If the document is a deed of transfer, verify that the property addresses and other key details are correct and in line with public records.

It's also important to ensure that the document is not being signed under duress or coercion, as mentioned earlier. If you notice any signs of distress or pressure from a third party, you should refuse to notarize the document.

## 3. Recognizing Red Flags

There are several red flags that can alert you to potential fraud or impersonation. It is important to remain vigilant during the notarization process and trust your instincts. Some common signs to look for include:

- **Inconsistent or Suspicious Behavior**: If the signer seems unusually nervous, avoids making eye contact, or exhibits erratic behavior, it could indicate that something is wrong. While nervousness alone is not an indication of fraud, if the behavior appears unusual or out of character, it's worth investigating further.
- **Discrepancies Between the Signer and the ID**: If the person presenting the ID does not match the individual in the document, or if the signer's physical appearance does not match the photo on the ID, it's a strong indicator that impersonation might be occurring. In such cases, ask the

signer to provide additional proof of their identity or request the assistance of a credible witness.

- **Unusual or Complex Documents**: Fraudsters sometimes use complex or unfamiliar legal documents to confuse notaries. If you encounter a document that seems complicated or involves unusual terms, take extra time to understand it. If you have any doubts, seek legal advice or consult with a professional in the relevant field.
- **Reluctance to Provide Identification**: If a signer is hesitant or refuses to provide identification, or if they insist on using expired or questionable forms of ID, this could be a sign of fraudulent intent. In such cases, it's critical to follow your professional standards and not proceed with the notarization.

### 4. Use of Technology and Databases

In today's digital age, notaries in California are increasingly relying on technology to help verify identities and prevent fraud. One such tool is the *Electronic Notary Journal*, which allows you to securely track the details of each notarization, including the type of ID presented and any additional information related to the signer's identity. By keeping a detailed electronic record, you create an audit trail that can be used to verify the authenticity of your notarial acts.

Additionally, notaries can use online databases to check the validity of certain types of documents or signatures. For example, you might be able to verify the authenticity of a document by checking public records or consulting with a title company in cases involving property transfers. Although the use of technology is not a substitute for performing a thorough in-person identity verification, it can be an added layer of protection.

### 5. Notarizing for the Right Parties

It's important to ensure that the signer is the correct person authorized to sign the document. Never allow a third party to sign on behalf of another individual unless you have clear, verifiable authorization, such as a *power of attorney*. Fraudulent transactions often involve individuals attempting to sign documents on behalf of someone else without permission. Before notarizing, confirm that the signer is authorized to act on behalf of any other parties involved.

Additionally, avoid notarizing documents for individuals who are not present or who you cannot personally verify. If someone asks you to notarize a document for someone who is absent or unavailable, politely refuse and explain that the signer must be physically present in front of you to complete the notarization.

### 6. Reporting Suspicious Activities

If you suspect fraudulent activity, you must take the appropriate steps to report the situation. In California, notaries are required by law to report certain crimes, including fraud or attempts at impersonation, to the authorities. If you encounter a situation where you believe a crime is being committed, contact local law enforcement or the appropriate regulatory body immediately.

In addition to contacting authorities, you should also document the incident in your notary journal. Record any relevant details, such as the date, time, nature of the situation, and any identifying information about the individuals involved. This documentation can help protect you in the event of a legal dispute.

Preventing fraudulent transactions and impersonations is a crucial aspect of your role as a notary public in California. By adhering to strict identity verification protocols, remaining vigilant for red flags, and following the proper procedures for notarizing documents, you can help protect your clients, yourself, and the integrity of the notarization process. Taking these precautions seriously not only ensures that you comply with the law, but also helps to maintain public trust in the notarial system as a whole. Always prioritize security, caution, and thoroughness in every transaction to minimize the risk of fraud and impersonation.

# CHAPTER 6
# SPECIAL CIRCUMSTANCES AND CHALLENGING SITUATIONS

## NOTARIZING FOR NON-ENGLISH SPEAKERS AND USE OF TRANSLATORS

As a notary public in California, one of the core responsibilities is ensuring that the signer understands the document they are signing and that they are doing so willingly and without coercion. This is the fundamental role of a notary – to act as an impartial witness to the signing of important legal documents. However, what happens when the signer does not speak English or is more comfortable using a different language? Notaries in California must be equipped with the knowledge of how to properly handle such situations, ensuring both the legality and integrity of the notarization process. This involves understanding the proper procedures when notarizing for non-English speakers, as well as how to use a translator or interpreter effectively while adhering to California notary laws.

**The Legal Requirements for Notarizing for Non-English Speakers**

California law requires that notaries must be able to communicate directly with the person whose signature they are witnessing. This ensures that the signer understands the contents of the document and is signing it of their own free will. If a signer does not speak English fluently, it can create a challenge for the notary, as both the signer and the notary need to have a mutual understanding of what is happening during the notarization.

When a non-English speaker appears before a notary, the notary must make sure that the signer fully understands the document they are about to sign. California law requires that the notary confirm that the signer understands what is written in the document, even if the signer cannot communicate in English. This can be accomplished by using a translator or interpreter to ensure clear communication. The primary legal concern in such cases is that the notary cannot allow the signer to sign a document they do not understand.

**Using a Translator or Interpreter**

California law allows the use of a third-party translator or interpreter to assist in the notarization process for non-English speakers. It is essential to note that the notary public cannot serve as the translator themselves if they do not speak the language fluently, as this could present a conflict of interest and undermine the impartiality of the notarization.

If a non-English speaking signer appears before you, and you cannot communicate with them in their language, you are permitted to use a *translator* or *interpreter* to facilitate the transaction. However, it is important that the translator is qualified to perform such a role. Ideally, the translator should be fluent in both English and the signer's language and should understand legal terminology to ensure accuracy in communication.

One thing to keep in mind is that the *translator* or *interpreter* must act solely as a conduit for the communication between you and the signer. They must not offer advice, make decisions on behalf of the signer, or influence the content of the document in any way. Their sole responsibility is to ensure that the signer fully understands the document they are about to sign.

It is also essential that the *translator* or *interpreter* be impartial. They should not have any personal interest in the transaction, nor should they be related to the signer or have any connection to the document being notarized. This helps ensure that the process is as transparent and unbiased as possible.

## The Notary's Role When Using a Translator or Interpreter

As a notary, it is your duty to ensure that the notarization process is carried out correctly, regardless of the language barriers involved. When using a translator or interpreter, you must follow specific procedures to ensure that the transaction remains legally valid. First and foremost, you must establish that the translator is competent and capable of conveying the document's contents accurately.

The role of the translator in this scenario is to ensure that both parties can understand each other, but the notary is still responsible for confirming the signer's identity and ensuring that the document is signed voluntarily and without duress. This means that you must be present and observe the entire process, even if you are not directly involved in the communication. It is your job to confirm that the translator is accurately conveying the signer's responses and understanding of the document.

Additionally, as part of your responsibility, you should take the time to ensure that the translation is clear and precise. The notary journal entry should also reflect the involvement of the translator or interpreter, including their name, contact information, and any other relevant details. This is essential for creating a clear record in the event that there are any questions about the notarization in the future.

## Journal Entry Requirements for Notarizing with a Translator

When notarizing for a non-English speaker using a translator, it is important to make sure that your notary journal includes the necessary information to document the use of the translator. In California, the notary public is required to record specific details about each notarization in their notary journal. When a translator is involved, the journal entry must reflect this fact.

Your journal entry should include:

- The name of the person using the translator.
- The name of the translator.
- A statement confirming that the document was read and explained to the signer by the translator.
- The type of document being notarized.
- A record of any other relevant information, such as the date, time, and location of the notarization.

These entries help protect both the notary and the signer by creating a transparent record of the notarization process. In the event of a dispute, your journal entry can serve as crucial evidence that all steps were taken properly.

**Recognizing and Avoiding Potential Issues**

While using a translator can help facilitate communication, there are certain issues to be aware of to avoid mistakes and potential legal risks. One key issue is the accuracy of the translation itself. If a translator makes an error in interpreting the document or the signer's responses, it could result in a situation where the signer is not fully aware of what they are signing. This could lead to a claim of fraud or coercion.

It is essential to ensure that the translator is qualified and trustworthy. The notary should ask for references or qualifications to verify the translator's competence, especially if the document being notarized is particularly complex or legally significant. A well-qualified translator will be able to translate not only the words but also the legal concepts, terms, and conditions within the document. If a translator is not able to do so, it may be necessary to find a different translator who is better equipped to handle the task.

Another issue to be aware of is the potential for *duress* or *coercion* when a translator is involved. Just as with any notarization, the notary must ensure that the signer is signing voluntarily and is not under any form of pressure or threat. If you suspect that the signer is being coerced by the translator or anyone else present, you should halt the notarization and take appropriate steps to protect the signer's rights.

**Special Considerations for Certain Documents**

Some documents may require additional considerations when being notarized for non-English speakers. For example, documents such as *wills*, *trusts*, and *powers of attorney* often contain complex legal language that may be difficult to translate accurately. In these cases, it is essential to ensure that the signer has a clear understanding of the content of the document before they sign it. The complexity of the language might require additional assistance from a legal professional or specialized translator to ensure the signer fully understands the legal implications.

Moreover, certain documents may have specific requirements regarding translations. For example, when a document is being notarized for a non-English speaker and is intended for use in a country outside the United States, there may be additional steps required, such as providing a certified translation of the document. In such cases, the notary should be aware of these requirements and guide the signer accordingly.

**Refusing to Notarize When Necessary**

As a notary, you have the right to refuse to notarize a document if you believe that the process cannot be completed properly or if you have concerns about the legality of the transaction. If a non-English speaker appears before you and there is no competent translator available, or if you feel that the signer does not fully understand the document, you should refuse to proceed with the notarization. It is crucial to prioritize accuracy, integrity, and compliance with the law.

Notarizing for non-English speakers is a responsibility that requires careful attention to detail and a strong understanding of legal and procedural requirements. By using competent translators and following the appropriate steps, you can help ensure that the notarization process is transparent, valid, and legally sound. Always make sure that the signer fully understands the document and is signing it voluntarily, and take the necessary precautions to protect both yourself and the signer from potential issues such as fraud or misunderstanding. By adhering to these principles, you can provide a crucial service to your clients while maintaining the highest standards of professionalism and legal compliance.

## HANDLING DOCUMENTS FOR THE ELDERLY OR DISABLED SIGNERS

As a notary public in California, you may occasionally encounter situations where the signer is elderly or disabled. Notarizing documents for these individuals requires a unique set of considerations to ensure that the process remains both legally sound and ethical. The elderly and disabled populations may face physical, cognitive, or sensory challenges that affect their ability to sign documents in a conventional manner. As a notary, it is important to approach these situations with sensitivity, understanding, and adherence to California's notary laws.

### Understanding the Special Needs of Elderly or Disabled Signers

When you encounter an elderly or disabled signer, it is crucial to first recognize that their challenges may not always be immediately visible. Disabilities can range from physical impairments, such as arthritis or limited mobility, to cognitive issues like dementia or memory loss. It is essential to approach each situation with empathy and flexibility, offering appropriate assistance while adhering to the notary's legal duties.

Some common challenges faced by elderly or disabled signers include:

- *Limited mobility* which may prevent the signer from physically attending the notarization or from signing the document themselves.
- *Cognitive impairments* that may make it difficult for the signer to fully comprehend the document or remember their intentions.
- *Vision or hearing impairments* that could make it challenging for the signer to read the document or hear the notary's instructions.
- *Speech impairments* that may prevent the signer from clearly communicating their intentions or understanding questions posed by the notary.

Understanding these potential challenges allows you to take the appropriate steps to ensure that the notarization is completed properly while preserving the integrity of the process.

### Ensuring Capacity to Understand and Sign the Document

Before proceeding with a notarization for an elderly or disabled signer, it is important to assess the signer's ability to understand the nature and consequences of the document they are about to sign. As a notary public, it is your responsibility to confirm that the signer is acting willingly and with full understanding. If there are any doubts about the signer's capacity to comprehend the document, the notarization should not proceed.

In California, notaries are legally required to ensure that the signer is mentally competent to enter into the transaction. If the signer has cognitive impairments such as dementia, Alzheimer's disease, or any form of memory loss, you must carefully assess whether they understand the purpose of the document and are signing it of their own free will. If you suspect that the signer does not fully comprehend the document due to their condition, it is your responsibility to stop the notarization process.

In some cases, a family member or legal guardian may be present to assist with the signer's understanding. However, you must still verify that the signer has the mental capacity to sign the document, even with assistance. If the signer is unable to understand the document, you should refuse to notarize it.

If a signer's ability to understand the document is in question, it may be appropriate to ask questions that help gauge their understanding. For example, you might ask the signer to explain what the document is for or to describe the general content of the document. If they are unable to do so, it may indicate a lack of capacity to sign. If you are unsure about the signer's mental capacity, you may want to seek guidance from a legal professional.

### Verifying Identity When Physical Limitations Are Present

In some cases, elderly or disabled signers may have physical limitations that affect their ability to provide traditional forms of identification, such as a driver's license or passport. It is important to remember that the notary's primary role is to verify the identity of the signer. If the signer cannot physically present their identification, you may need to explore alternative methods to verify their identity.

California law allows the notary to use a credible witness in situations where the signer is unable to provide proper identification. A credible witness is a person who personally knows the signer and can vouch for their identity. The credible witness must swear an oath before the notary and must have valid identification of their own.

It is also important to note that some elderly or disabled individuals may have legal guardians or caregivers who assist with their personal affairs. If a guardian or caregiver is involved, they can act as the credible witness, provided they meet the necessary requirements. However, it is important that the notary ensures that the guardian or caregiver has no vested interest in the document being notarized and does not stand to benefit from the transaction.

In cases where a signer is unable to provide proper identification due to physical or cognitive impairments, the notary should always adhere to the strict guidelines set forth by California law and may need to work with legal professionals or caregivers to verify the identity of the signer.

### Assisting with the Signing Process

For elderly or disabled signers, the physical act of signing a document may be challenging. Notaries should approach this situation with patience and care, while remaining within the legal parameters of their duties.

If the signer is physically unable to sign the document due to mobility issues or limited dexterity, there are a few options available:

- The signer may choose to use a *signature by mark*. In this case, the signer marks the document with an "X" or other symbol that represents their signature. The notary must witness the mark and record in the notary journal that the signer signed by mark due to physical limitations.

- In cases where the signer cannot physically mark the document themselves, the notary may assist the signer by *signing the document on their behalf* if specifically requested to do so. This should only occur when the signer has given their explicit consent and it is noted in the notary journal.

It is important that the notary does not sign the document on behalf of the signer unless specifically requested to do so, and the request must be noted in the notary journal. Additionally, the notary must ensure that the signer is fully aware of what is happening during the signing process, even if they are unable to sign the document themselves.

In situations where the signer is unable to physically sign or mark the document, it is crucial to ensure that there is a proper witness to the process, particularly if a *signature by mark* is used. The notary should document the process in the notary journal, including details of the signer's condition and the method used for signing the document.

### Providing Extra Care to the Elderly or Disabled Signer

In some cases, elderly or disabled signers may require additional assistance or accommodations to ensure that the notarization is conducted smoothly. Notaries must be prepared to provide such accommodations, all while adhering to the legal requirements of the notarization process.

Some general practices to follow when assisting elderly or disabled signers include:

- Ensuring a *quiet, comfortable environment* for the signer to reduce distractions and stress. This can be especially important if the signer has hearing or vision impairments.

- Offering assistance with *document reading* for signers who have difficulty seeing or reading the document due to age or disability. This might involve reading the document aloud or arranging for someone to assist in reading.

- Providing additional time for the signer to process the information, especially if they are experiencing memory loss or confusion. It is important to avoid rushing the process to ensure that the signer fully understands the document they are signing.

Notaries should also be aware of the need for *empathy* when working with elderly or disabled signers. The notarization process can be stressful for individuals who may already be dealing with health issues or challenges related to aging or disability. Taking the time to explain the process, reassure the signer, and offer appropriate assistance can go a long way in ensuring that the notarization is completed correctly and without undue pressure.

**Documenting the Process in the Notary Journal**

The notary journal plays an essential role in documenting the notarization process, especially when it involves elderly or disabled signers. The notary should make a detailed journal entry, noting any relevant circumstances that may have affected the process. This includes:

- The signer's condition, if it is relevant (e.g., if the signer was physically or cognitively impaired).
- The method used for signing, such as *signature by mark* or assistance in signing.
- The use of any third parties, such as *caregivers* or *guardians*, who may have been present to assist the signer.

Proper documentation helps protect both the signer and the notary, and it provides a clear record of the notarization process should any questions arise in the future.

**Ethical Considerations and Legal Responsibilities**

While notaries are not expected to act as legal advisors, it is important to approach notarizations for elderly or disabled signers with an awareness of potential ethical concerns. For example, elderly individuals are sometimes vulnerable to *financial exploitation* or *fraud*, and it is the notary's responsibility to remain vigilant for any signs that the signer may be under duress or acting against their best interests. If you have any concerns that the signer is being pressured or coerced into signing a document, you must refuse to perform the notarization and report the situation to the proper authorities.

It is also essential that the notary ensures the signer's *voluntary* participation in the notarization process. Any signs of undue influence, manipulation, or coercion should be addressed immediately, and the notarization should be halted if any of these concerns arise.

Handling documents for elderly or disabled signers requires a careful balance of legal knowledge, sensitivity, and patience. By understanding the special needs of these individuals and adhering to California's notary laws, you can ensure that the notarization process is completed correctly, ethically, and with the respect that every signer deserves.

## REMOTE ONLINE NOTARIZATION: CURRENT STATUS AND FUTURE TRENDS

Remote Online Notarization (RON) is a relatively recent development in the field of notarization, and its impact on the notary profession has been substantial, especially in the context of the ever-evolving digital landscape. As technology continues to advance, RON presents a revolutionary way to perform notarizations that are more accessible, efficient, and secure than ever before. For California notaries, understanding the current status of RON, its legal implications, and the future trends that are shaping this new mode of notarization is essential for staying ahead in a rapidly changing industry.

Remote Online Notarization is the process by which a notary public witnesses the signing of a document remotely, using audio-visual technology, rather than in person. This digital process enables signers and notaries to interact in real-time via a secure platform, with all required identification verification and document signing taking place electronically. RON has gained considerable attention in recent years, particularly during the COVID-19 pandemic, when the demand for remote services skyrocketed due to social distancing requirements and the increased reliance on digital transactions.

For California notaries, this shift towards a more digital and remote way of conducting notarizations means new opportunities but also new responsibilities and legal considerations. As the demand for RON grows, it is critical for notaries to understand not only the technical aspects of performing RON but also the evolving legal landscape that surrounds it.

### The Legal Framework of Remote Online Notarization in California

Before delving into the specific technical requirements and processes of RON, it is important to establish the legal framework that governs this practice in California. As of January 1, 2020, California enacted Assembly Bill 1096, which authorized Remote Online Notarization in the state. The bill brought California into alignment with the growing national trend of recognizing RON as a legitimate form of notarization. However, the legal parameters surrounding RON are nuanced and require a thorough understanding to ensure compliance.

California's approach to RON requires a notary to perform notarizations using an approved platform that meets the state's security and identity verification requirements. One of the key elements of California's RON process is that notaries must utilize a platform that has been specifically authorized by the Secretary of State. These platforms must adhere to strict security protocols that protect against fraud and ensure the integrity of the notarization process.

California law requires that the notary confirm the identity of the signer using multi-factor authentication methods before performing any notarization. These methods typically involve a combination of credential analysis (such as verifying government-issued identification) and identity proofing through knowledge-based authentication (such as answering personal questions that only the signer would know). The signer must also use a webcam or similar video technology to appear before the notary in real-time, enabling the notary to observe the signing process and ensure that it is taking place voluntarily and without coercion.

The notarization process must be recorded and securely stored for a period of at least five years, in accordance with California's regulations. These recordings provide an additional layer of security and serve as proof that the notarization was conducted in accordance with the law.

One critical aspect to note is that not all documents are eligible for remote notarization in California. Certain legal documents, such as wills, powers of attorney for health care, and documents requiring an in-person presence, are excluded from the RON process. Notaries must be aware of these restrictions to avoid inadvertently performing an unauthorized notarization.

**Performing Remote Online Notarization**

Performing a Remote Online Notarization is similar to performing a traditional notarization in many ways, but it does require familiarity with the technology and the digital process involved. First and foremost, the notary must ensure that they are using an authorized and compliant RON platform. The platform must be equipped with tools to handle the video conference, document upload and signing, and identity verification processes.

Once the platform is set up and the signer has joined the session, the notary must verify the signer's identity. This is done through multi-factor authentication, which may include confirming the signer's identification document through visual analysis, asking knowledge-based questions, and analyzing biometric features like facial recognition. After the identity has been verified, the notary can proceed with the document signing. The signer must sign the document electronically on the platform, and the notary can then apply their electronic signature and seal to the document.

One unique aspect of RON is the ability to track the entire process electronically. Notaries must also record the transaction, including the video session, to ensure compliance with the law. These recordings are stored securely on the RON platform for future reference, which can be helpful if the notarization is ever called into question.

Once the notarization is complete, the notary will typically provide the signer with a digital version of the notarized document. The notarized document can then be distributed electronically, sent to other parties involved in the transaction, or printed as needed.

**The Advantages of Remote Online Notarization**

Remote Online Notarization offers numerous benefits for notaries and signers alike. One of the primary advantages is convenience. RON allows notaries to perform notarizations from anywhere, as long as they have access to an authorized platform and the necessary technology. This flexibility is especially beneficial for notaries who may not have a fixed office or who work with clients across a wide geographic area.

For signers, the ability to complete a notarization remotely offers significant time savings and eliminates the need for in-person meetings. This can be particularly advantageous for individuals with mobility issues, those who live in rural or remote areas, or individuals who have busy schedules that make in-person notarizations difficult to arrange. Furthermore, remote notarizations can be conducted at any time, not limited by regular business hours, providing greater flexibility for both the notary and the signer.

Additionally, RON can help to reduce the risk of fraud and errors. Since the process relies heavily on secure technology and identity verification, it offers an added layer of protection against impersonation and other forms of fraud. The use of real-time video allows the notary to observe the signer's actions, helping to ensure that the transaction is being conducted voluntarily and that the signer understands the nature of the document being signed.

### The Challenges of Remote Online Notarization

While the advantages of Remote Online Notarization are clear, there are also several challenges and limitations associated with this practice. One significant challenge is the technology barrier. Not all signers may have access to the necessary technology, such as a computer or smartphone with a webcam and a reliable internet connection. For some, the process may be intimidating or confusing, requiring additional guidance from the notary to complete the notarization successfully.

Another challenge is the legal uncertainty surrounding the use of RON across state lines. While California has authorized Remote Online Notarization, the legal landscape for RON varies significantly from state to state. Some states have not yet passed laws allowing RON, while others may have different requirements for identity verification and document handling. As a result, notaries may face challenges when dealing with documents from other states or signers who are located outside of California. It is essential for California notaries to stay informed about the legal status of RON in other states and to be aware of any specific regulations that may apply to out-of-state transactions.

### The Future of Remote Online Notarization

The future of Remote Online Notarization appears promising, with increasing adoption across the United States and a growing demand for digital notarization services. As technology continues to advance, the tools and platforms used for RON are likely to become even more sophisticated, offering enhanced security features, improved user experiences, and more seamless integration with other digital systems.

One area where RON is expected to grow is in the real estate industry. As more real estate transactions are conducted remotely, the demand for online notarizations will continue to rise. Additionally, as more businesses and individuals become accustomed to conducting transactions digitally, the need for remote notarizations will expand beyond traditional legal documents, covering a wide range of industries and transactions.

California is likely to continue playing a leading role in the development of Remote Online Notarization, with the state's government and regulators focusing on refining the legal framework and ensuring that RON practices remain secure, reliable, and accessible. As the technology improves and more notaries become familiar with RON platforms, the process may become more standardized, making it easier for notaries to adopt and integrate into their daily workflows.

As the notary profession continues to evolve, remote online notarization is poised to become an integral part of the industry. By embracing RON, notaries can expand their service offerings, increase their client base, and stay ahead of emerging trends in the notary world. However, as with any new technology, it is important to stay informed about the latest developments, legal requirements, and best practices to ensure that your remote notarizations are performed accurately, securely, and in compliance with California law.

## DEALING WITH REFUSAL OF NOTARIAL SERVICES

Dealing with the refusal of notarial services is one of the more delicate aspects of being a notary public in California. As a notary, you are entrusted with the responsibility to carry out specific duties in accordance with state law, ensuring that legal documents are notarized properly and securely. However, not all situations will be straightforward, and there may be times when you must refuse to provide notarial services to a signer. Understanding the legal grounds for refusal, the proper procedures to follow, and how to handle these situations professionally is essential for maintaining your integrity and protecting both your notary commission and the interests of your clients.

**Legal Grounds for Refusal**

As a California notary public, you are not required to notarize a document in every instance. There are specific legal grounds outlined in California law under which you may refuse to notarize a document. Knowing these grounds thoroughly will ensure that you act within the scope of your authority and avoid inadvertently engaging in any illegal activities.

The first and foremost reason to refuse notarization is *lack of proper identification*. California law mandates that the signer must be personally known to the notary or must present valid identification that meets the legal standards. If the signer cannot produce proper identification or if you, as the notary, have doubts about the authenticity of the ID, you must refuse to notarize the document. It is important that you ensure the identification is not expired and is from an acceptable list of documents, such as a state-issued driver's license or a passport.

Another common reason for refusal is if the signer is unable to understand the document. If the signer does not comprehend the nature of the document they are signing, due to language barriers, mental incapacity, or any other reason, it is your duty to refuse notarization. The California Notary Handbook specifies that a notary may not perform a notarial act if the signer appears to be *under duress* or coerced into signing. If you have any reason to believe that the signer does not understand the document or that they are being forced to sign it, you must refuse the notarization.

The third scenario involves *incomplete documents*. A notary is only permitted to notarize a document that is complete, meaning that all required sections are filled out before the notarization occurs. If the document is blank or missing essential information, such as dates, names, or other critical elements, it is not acceptable for notarization. A notary must verify that the document is fully completed before proceeding.

In cases where you have *personal interest* in the transaction, either directly or indirectly, you are required to refuse notarizing the document. This is to prevent conflicts of interest and ensure that notarizations are carried out impartially. For example, if you stand to benefit from the document being notarized, such as being named in a will or involved in a business transaction, you must avoid notarizing that document. California law prohibits notaries from acting in situations where their impartiality is in question.

Lastly, if the document being presented involves illegal or fraudulent activities, a notary must refuse notarization. While this may seem straightforward, it's important to be aware of potential red flags. If you suspect that the document could be used to facilitate fraud, such as a forged signature or an invalid power of attorney, you must refuse to proceed with the notarization.

**Handling the Refusal Process**

While it is within your legal rights to refuse to notarize a document for any of the reasons mentioned above, handling the refusal in a professional and respectful manner is essential. When refusing a notarization, you must do so in a way that avoids confrontation or misunderstanding. Notaries are often seen as impartial witnesses, and maintaining that impartiality is crucial, especially when denying services.

Begin by clearly explaining the reason for the refusal. If the issue is a lack of identification, calmly inform the signer that you are unable to proceed without proper identification. If the signer does not understand the document, kindly explain that you are unable to notarize documents when the signer is not fully aware of the contents or consequences of the document. If the signer seems to be under duress or appears to be coerced, politely explain that you cannot notarize documents if there is any indication that the signer is being forced into signing.

In some cases, the signer may become frustrated or upset. It is essential to stay calm and respectful. Avoid arguing with the signer or providing any legal advice. Acknowledge their concerns but stick to the facts and the law. If necessary, offer to explain the process further or refer them to another notary who may be able to help once the issue is resolved.

For example, if a signer refuses to provide a valid ID, you might say, "I understand that this situation may be inconvenient, but I am required by California law to confirm the identity of the signer. Unfortunately, I am unable to notarize the document without proper identification."

If you refuse notarization because of the signer's inability to understand the document or if you suspect that the document could be used for fraudulent purposes, it is important to maintain a professional tone. It is not your role to judge the signer's character but to follow the law. If the signer is not aware of the implications of the document they are signing or if you feel that they are being pressured, politely explain that you cannot proceed with the notarization under those circumstances. For example, you could say, "For your protection, I must ensure that you understand the document fully before notarizing it. If you feel you need more time to review or understand the content, I can help you find resources or provide you with some time to gather your thoughts."

**Documentation of the Refusal**

In California, notaries are required to keep detailed records of all notarial acts they perform in their journal. This includes situations where a notarization is refused. It is vital to document the reason for refusal in your notary journal as a safeguard against potential legal challenges. The refusal must be recorded clearly and accurately, with a note of the date, time, and reason for refusal. If the refusal is based on an issue such as lack of identification or the signer's inability to comprehend the document, make sure to record that information.

Keeping a thorough record not only ensures compliance with California law but also protects you from any future liability. If a document or transaction comes into question, having a comprehensive journal entry showing the reason for refusal can provide a strong defense.

For example, if you refused notarization because the signer did not have proper ID, your journal entry could read: "Refused notarization on 05/12/2025 due to lack of valid identification." Similarly, if you refused due to suspicion of coercion or duress, you could document: "Refused notarization on 05/12/2025 due to concern of duress, signer appeared pressured and did not demonstrate understanding."

**Consequences of Improper Refusal**

As a notary public in California, you are empowered to refuse a notarization when necessary, but improper refusals can lead to serious consequences. If you refuse notarization for invalid or unjust reasons, you could be held liable for any resulting damages or legal actions. Additionally, if your refusal violates any part of your notarial duties, you risk losing your notary commission, facing legal repercussions, or facing a complaint before the California Secretary of State.

For example, if you refuse to notarize a document without a valid reason, such as rejecting a valid ID without cause, the signer could file a complaint, and you could face disciplinary action. In this case, the notary could also be held liable if the signer suffers financial harm due to not being able to execute the necessary document. It is therefore important that refusals are handled professionally, and based on sound legal grounds.

Dealing with refusals of notarial services is an important aspect of a notary's responsibilities. Understanding the legal grounds for refusal and ensuring that you follow the proper procedures can help protect both yourself and the signers you serve. It's essential to handle refusals with professionalism and empathy, providing clear explanations and maintaining your role as a neutral and impartial witness. Refusing notarial services may not always be easy, but by adhering to California law and keeping thorough records, you ensure that you are acting in accordance with your duties while protecting the integrity of the notarial process.

# CHAPTER 7
## ETHICS AND PROFESSIONAL CONDUCT

### ETHICAL PRINCIPLES GOVERNING NOTARIAL PRACTICE

As a notary public in California, your responsibilities extend far beyond simply witnessing signatures and administering oaths. You are held to a higher standard of professionalism and ethics, and your actions can have significant legal consequences for both you and those you serve. Ethical principles governing notarial practice are foundational to ensuring that notaries uphold the integrity of the notarial process. Understanding these principles, adhering to them, and conducting yourself with the utmost professionalism is not just about protecting your notary commission but also about maintaining public trust and confidence in the notarial system.

Ethics in notarial practice can be understood as a combination of legal requirements, professional standards, and personal integrity. These principles are essential in shaping the way you interact with clients, document signers, and the legal system. When performing your duties, you must be impartial, honest, and transparent, and act in accordance with the law to prevent fraud and ensure that notarizations are carried out correctly.

One of the most important ethical principles you must follow is *impartiality*. As a notary, you are an impartial witness to the signing of documents, and your role is to verify the identities of the signers, ensure they understand the documents, and confirm that they are signing voluntarily. You must not take sides, show favoritism, or provide legal advice to any party involved. If you have a personal or financial interest in the transaction or if you are related to the signer, you should not notarize the document. Impartiality is the cornerstone of notarial ethics, as your presence is meant to protect all parties by ensuring that the document is executed properly and without undue influence.

Another key ethical principle is *honesty and transparency*. As a notary, you are expected to be truthful in your actions, including documenting your notarial acts and accurately recording the details in your notary journal. Misrepresenting information, falsifying records, or failing to document the facts of the transaction can lead to serious legal consequences, including the loss of your notary commission, legal action, and even criminal charges. Being transparent also means clearly communicating the notarial process to the signer, ensuring they understand what you are doing and why. For example, if a signer is unsure about the type of document they are signing, it is your responsibility to inform them that you cannot provide legal advice but that you are only witnessing their signature. Transparency builds trust and reduces the potential for misunderstandings.

*Confidentiality* is another crucial ethical consideration for notaries. When notarizing documents, you may have access to sensitive information such as names, addresses, financial details, and personal matters. It is your duty to protect this information and prevent it from being disclosed without the signer's consent, except in cases where the law requires disclosure. This means that you must not share the contents of a notarized document with third parties, unless you are legally obligated to do so. Maintaining confidentiality fosters trust between you and your clients and upholds the integrity of the notarial process.

Furthermore, you must adhere to the principle of *competence*. To be competent, you must possess the necessary knowledge and skills to perform notarial acts correctly and in compliance with California law. This includes understanding the procedures for verifying the identity of signers, knowing how to properly administer oaths or affirmations, and recognizing the types of documents you are authorized to notarize. Incompetence in handling notarial acts can result in mistakes that may affect the validity of documents or lead to legal disputes. To maintain your competence, it is essential that you stay informed about changes in California notary laws and best practices. Attending notary education courses and regularly reviewing official notary guidelines will help ensure that you can effectively fulfill your duties.

You must also be aware of the principle of *avoidance of conflicts of interest*. Notaries are prohibited from notarizing documents in which they have a personal or financial interest. This prohibition helps ensure that notarizations are not influenced by personal gain or bias. For example, you should not notarize a document in which you stand to benefit, such as a will or a business agreement in which you are involved. Conflicts of interest undermine the impartiality of the notarial process and can lead to questions about the legitimacy of the notarization.

*Due diligence* is another important aspect of ethical practice. When performing notarial acts, you must take reasonable steps to ensure that the transaction is legitimate. This means verifying the identity of the signer, ensuring that they are signing the document voluntarily, and confirming that they understand the contents of the document. If you have any concerns about the authenticity of the transaction or if you suspect fraud, you should not proceed with the notarization. Your role is to protect the integrity of the document-signing process, and due diligence is a vital component of that responsibility. If you suspect that the signer is under duress, or if the document appears to be forged or altered, you must refuse to notarize it and report any concerns to the appropriate authorities.

In some cases, you may be required to refuse notarization due to the *inability of the signer to understand the document* or the notarial act. For instance, if the signer is unable to comprehend the language of the document, has impaired mental faculties, or cannot communicate effectively, it is your duty to refuse the notarization. Notarizing a document for someone who cannot understand it, even with the help of an interpreter, could lead to serious consequences, including charges of fraud or misconduct. It is also important to be cautious when notarizing documents for individuals who may be under the influence of alcohol or drugs, as their ability to sign the document knowingly and voluntarily could be compromised. In these situations, you must exercise your best judgment and refuse notarization if you believe that the signer is not acting with full mental clarity.

The principle of *responsibility* also applies to notaries in California. You are responsible for understanding the full scope of your duties and acting in compliance with the laws and regulations governing notarial acts. This means that you must keep accurate records, such as maintaining a notary journal that documents the details of each notarization. Your journal serves as a public record of your notarial activities, and you are obligated to provide access to it when requested by authorized individuals, such as law enforcement officials or other regulatory bodies. Keeping detailed records helps ensure that notarizations are properly documented and can be verified in case of legal disputes.

In addition to these ethical principles, notaries must also be mindful of the *potential for fraud and exploitation* within their practice. Fraudulent activities can undermine the legitimacy of notarizations and have severe consequences for both the notary and the parties involved. For example, if a signer provides false information or signs a document under false pretenses, it is your responsibility to identify and address the situation before proceeding with the notarization. If you suspect that a signer is attempting to commit fraud, you must refuse to notarize the document and report your suspicions to the relevant authorities.

Moreover, as a notary, you must ensure that you do not inadvertently become involved in fraudulent practices. For example, it is unethical and illegal to allow someone else to sign a document on behalf of another person without proper authorization. This includes situations where a signer may ask you to notarize a document that is blank or incomplete. You must refuse to notarize any document that is not fully completed or that contains blank spaces. Allowing such documents to be notarized opens the door to potential fraud and places both you and your clients at risk.

Finally, it is essential for notaries to maintain a strong sense of *professionalism* in their practice. This includes treating clients with respect, being punctual, and ensuring that your notarial services are provided in a clean and professional setting. A notary's reputation is one of their most valuable assets, and maintaining professionalism helps to build trust and confidence among clients. Furthermore, you should ensure that your notary seal is properly maintained, stored securely, and used only in accordance with California law.

Adhering to ethical principles in notarial practice is essential for maintaining the integrity of the notarial process and protecting both the notary and the public. By remaining impartial, honest, transparent, and responsible, you help to ensure that notarizations are performed correctly and legally, and you contribute to the overall trust in the notarial system. Your role as a notary is an important one, and by upholding the highest ethical standards, you can continue to serve your community with professionalism and integrity.

## AVOIDING CONFLICTS OF INTEREST

As a notary public in California, it is crucial to uphold the integrity of your role by avoiding any potential conflicts of interest. Notaries are expected to serve as impartial witnesses who confirm the authenticity of signatures and the voluntary nature of document signings. The core principle of impartiality is essential to maintaining the legitimacy of the notarial process, and any appearance of conflict of interest can undermine public trust and jeopardize the validity of the notarization. A conflict of interest occurs when a notary has a personal or financial interest in a transaction, or when the notary's objectivity could reasonably be called into question due to personal relationships or other factors.

The most basic rule regarding conflicts of interest is that a notary must never notarize a document in which they have a *personal interest*. This can range from having a direct financial stake in the document or transaction, to being closely related to one of the parties involved in the notarization. Such conflicts can create a situation where a notary may feel pressured or biased, intentionally or unintentionally, to act in a way that benefits one party over another. This compromises the notary's duty to serve as a neutral and impartial witness. If a notary is in any way personally involved or stands to gain from the notarization, it is important to refuse the notarial act altogether.

Consider a situation in which a notary is asked to notarize a business contract that they are personally invested in, either as a partner in the business or as a stakeholder in the agreement. In such cases, the notary is disqualified from performing the notarization because their personal financial interest could compromise their neutrality. The same principle applies when a notary is asked to notarize a document for a family member, such as a will or power of attorney. Even if the notary believes they are unbiased and capable of remaining neutral, the mere appearance of a conflict of interest can make the notarization invalid and potentially open the door for challenges to the document's authenticity.

California law specifically prohibits notaries from notarizing documents in which they have a *direct or indirect interest*. A direct interest is an obvious personal or financial stake in the document or transaction. An indirect interest might involve situations where the notary has a close personal relationship with one of the signers or parties involved, such as being the best friend of one of the individuals signing a will. While the notary may feel they are impartial, the close relationship could make it difficult for them to remain completely neutral, which could give rise to questions about the document's validity. Even the appearance of a conflict of interest can lead to legal challenges or complications.

Moreover, the notary must be cautious when a signer or another party attempts to exert undue influence or pressure on them. If a signer is urging the notary to act in a way that benefits one party, even if the notary's interest is not directly tied to the transaction, this could create a subtle but significant conflict of interest. In these cases, the notary should maintain their objectivity and refuse to proceed with the notarization if they feel they are being unduly influenced. It is essential for the notary to resist any form of pressure, whether from friends, family, or clients, and to prioritize their duty to perform impartial, unbiased notarial acts. Even when the notary feels confident in their ability to remain neutral, any outside influence can raise doubts about the fairness and integrity of the process.

In addition to avoiding personal interests, notaries must also steer clear of notarizing documents when they have any involvement in the *content of the document*. For instance, if a notary is asked to notarize a contract that they helped draft or reviewed, they are disqualified from performing the notarization. This is because they are no longer serving as an impartial witness—they have a vested interest in the content of the document and may have influenced its terms. Even if the notary did not directly contribute to the document, their involvement in its creation can create a perception of bias. Therefore, a notary should always avoid any situation where they are closely associated with the content of the document.

Similarly, if a notary has been given access to information about a private transaction—such as the details of a confidential legal matter, or the terms of a business deal—they should refrain from notarizing any documents related to that matter. A notary's role is to witness the signing and verify the identity of the signers, not to engage in or have knowledge of the details of the transaction. Having access to sensitive information can compromise the notary's impartiality, as they may inadvertently form opinions or develop preferences regarding the transaction. To avoid the appearance of a conflict of interest, notaries should decline to notarize any document related to a transaction where they have knowledge beyond the scope of the notarization itself.

It is also important to recognize situations where a notary might be asked to notarize a document for a *close family member*, such as a spouse, child, parent, or sibling. While California law does not explicitly prohibit notarizing documents for family members, it is considered a best practice to avoid such transactions when possible. The potential for conflict of interest is high because of the personal relationship, which could lead to questions about the impartiality of the notary. For instance, a signer may feel pressured to proceed with a notarization simply because the notary is a family member, and that pressure could undermine the voluntary nature of the signing. To avoid even the appearance of a conflict of interest, it is generally advisable to seek out another notary for family-related notarizations. If this is not possible, the notary should take extra care to ensure that all requirements are met, including verifying that the signer is acting of their own free will.

In some cases, a notary may be asked to notarize documents related to a *transaction involving multiple parties*. These situations can be particularly complex when there are multiple signers with differing interests. For example, a notary may be asked to notarize a deed of trust involving a borrower and lender. In this case, the notary must remain impartial and ensure that both parties fully understand the document and are signing voluntarily. If the notary has a relationship with one of the parties, they must avoid any involvement in the notarization, as it may create a conflict of interest.

California law also prohibits notaries from performing *notarial acts in situations where they may have a conflict due to a prior professional relationship*. For example, if a notary has previously represented one of the parties involved in a legal dispute, they should not notarize documents related to that dispute. Even if the notary is no longer involved in the case, the history of the relationship may raise questions about their impartiality. To ensure that the notarization is beyond reproach, it is best for the notary to avoid performing notarial acts for individuals with whom they have had a prior business or professional relationship, particularly when the transaction involves sensitive or high-stakes matters.

When a notary is confronted with a situation where a conflict of interest may arise, it is important to err on the side of caution and refuse the notarial act. While it may seem inconvenient or uncomfortable, protecting the integrity of the notarial process is of utmost importance. If you find yourself in a situation where a conflict of interest is possible, explain to the signer that, in accordance with California law and professional ethics, you are unable to notarize the document. There is no shame in turning down a notarization when you suspect a potential conflict of interest, and doing so will help protect your reputation and ensure the legal validity of the document.

Moreover, notaries must maintain *proper documentation* of each notarization to safeguard themselves against any future claims of conflict of interest or misconduct. By keeping a detailed journal of all notarial acts, including information about the signers, the documents involved, and the circumstances surrounding the notarization, a notary can demonstrate that they followed proper procedures and adhered to ethical standards. This record can be invaluable in case questions arise about the impartiality of a notarization, as it provides a clear, verifiable account of the notary's actions.

Avoiding conflicts of interest is a fundamental aspect of notarial practice in California. Notaries must always prioritize impartiality, objectivity, and transparency to ensure that their actions are above reproach. By understanding what constitutes a conflict of interest and exercising caution in every notarization, you can uphold the integrity of the notarial process and protect both your clients and yourself from potential legal issues. Notarizations must be carried out with the highest level of professionalism, and avoiding conflicts of interest is a key part of maintaining public trust in the notarial system.

## ADVERTISING AND THE USE OF FOREIGN LANGUAGE TRANSLATIONS

When you take on the responsibility of becoming a notary public in California, your professional reputation and credibility are paramount to your success. One of the key areas that notaries need to be cautious about is how they advertise their services and the use of foreign language translations. While advertising is a legitimate means of reaching potential clients, there are strict rules and guidelines in place to ensure that notaries do not mislead the public or engage in any activity that may harm the integrity of the notarial process. It is essential to understand the regulations that govern advertising for notaries and the potential pitfalls involved when dealing with foreign language translations.

First and foremost, when advertising your notarial services, whether it be through print, digital platforms, or signage, you must always be transparent about the specific services you provide and avoid any deceptive or misleading claims. Notaries in California are not permitted to advertise that they can offer legal advice or legal services. While you may be highly knowledgeable about the notarial process, your role as a notary does not include providing legal guidance. It is critical to understand that a notary's job is to verify signatures, administer oaths, and perform other duties associated with notarization, but not to interpret or explain legal documents to clients. Therefore, any advertisements that suggest otherwise can mislead potential clients and are considered unethical and illegal.

For example, if a notary advertises their services as offering "legal advice" or "assistance with legal documents," they could face disciplinary actions, including the loss of their notary commission. California law clearly prohibits notaries from using language that implies they are authorized to practice law unless they are a licensed attorney. It is essential to make it clear that your services are limited to notarizing documents and that you are not authorized to offer legal counsel. Additionally, advertising that you can perform services outside the scope of notarial duties, such as assisting with the preparation of legal forms or documents, is also a violation of the law. These types of misleading statements can be detrimental to your professional standing and may even lead to lawsuits or legal consequences.

When considering how to advertise your services, it is also essential to be mindful of the medium through which you choose to promote your notary business. You should be careful when using platforms that allow you to target specific groups or communities, especially if you're offering your services in areas with a high concentration of non-English speakers. Although it is perfectly fine to advertise in these communities, the language used in the advertisement must still adhere to legal standards. For example, if you are targeting a Spanish-speaking community and wish to advertise your notarial services, you must ensure that your advertisement is clear, concise, and truthful. Offering advertisements in foreign languages is not inherently problematic; however, it becomes a concern when the translation is inaccurate or misleading.

In California, if you advertise your notarial services in a language other than English, you must ensure that the translation is both *accurate* and *clear*. Misleading or faulty translations can cause confusion and may result in complaints or legal action. Inaccurate translations can easily lead to misunderstandings, and when clients are confused or unclear about what services are being offered, it compromises their trust and confidence in the notarial process. For instance, if you were to advertise your services as "providing legal advice" in Spanish when this is not the case, you could face serious consequences under California law. Ensuring that translations are precise and properly reflect the actual scope of your services is not only legally required but is also a reflection of your professionalism and commitment to serving your community.

To further ensure clarity and avoid any issues with foreign language advertising, notaries in California are also required to adhere to specific language guidelines when performing notarial acts in a foreign language. If you are providing services to clients who do not speak English, it is important to be aware that the notarial certificate should be in English. This is because California law mandates that the notarial certificate must be written in English, even if the documents being notarized are in another language. If the signers do not understand English, you must make sure that they are fully aware of what they are signing and that the notarization process is carried out correctly.

If you are asked to notarize a document in a foreign language for a signer who does not speak English, the signer may have difficulty understanding the notarial certificate itself, as it will be written in English. To assist them, you may need to rely on a *qualified interpreter* to explain the document to them in their native language. The interpreter must be impartial and capable of providing an accurate translation. The interpreter must also sign a declaration stating that they have provided an accurate translation to the signer. This ensures that the notarial process is carried out with the full consent and understanding of the signer, which is an essential element of the notarization process.

When it comes to advertising, many notaries find themselves facing the challenge of ensuring that their advertisements reach the right audience while remaining compliant with the law. If you decide to advertise your services in multiple languages, you must be especially diligent in ensuring that all content, both in English and in other languages, is truthful and accurate. Any discrepancies between the English-language content of your advertisement and a foreign-language translation could lead to confusion and misunderstandings, which is a serious problem in the field of notarization. An advertisement that may appear harmless in one language could be interpreted completely differently in another, so great care must be taken to ensure consistency and accuracy across all platforms and languages.

Furthermore, California law has established specific rules for how notaries can use their title in advertising. As a notary public, you must be cautious about how you represent yourself in your advertisements. You are only allowed to refer to yourself as a "Notary Public" or "Notary" in a way that reflects your actual role and responsibilities. Using terms such as "Notary Specialist" or "Notary Expert" is prohibited, as it can imply that you possess specialized qualifications that go beyond your notarial duties. Being transparent about your role as a notary public helps protect both your clients and your professional reputation.

In addition to being mindful of your language and title usage, you must also be cautious about offering notarial services that are specifically prohibited by law. For example, while you are permitted to advertise general notarial services, you must never offer to act as a *document preparer* or assist in the drafting of documents. Document preparation is a separate profession and can only be performed by a licensed attorney or a licensed legal document assistant. Therefore, you should never offer to assist in preparing documents for clients or advertise that you can help clients fill out forms, as this could lead to legal repercussions and damage your reputation.

One key aspect to remember when advertising your notary services is the importance of following ethical guidelines at all times. These guidelines are in place to ensure that your clients receive the highest level of service while also protecting the integrity of the notarial process. If you find yourself in a situation where you are unsure whether an advertisement or translation is compliant with California law, it is always best to consult with a legal expert or seek guidance from the California Secretary of State's office. By doing so, you ensure that you are abiding by all the rules, providing clarity to your clients, and safeguarding your notary commission.

When you advertise your notary services, particularly in a foreign language, it is important to remain transparent, truthful, and clear about the services you offer. The use of foreign language translations can help you reach a broader audience, but accuracy is paramount in maintaining the integrity of your advertising and your notarial services. Misleading advertisements, even if unintentional, can lead to legal consequences and tarnish your professional standing. Always prioritize clarity and ensure that your advertising reflects the scope of your duties as a notary public in California.

## LEGAL CONSEQUENCES OF MISCONDUCT AND NEGLIGENCE

As a notary public in California, your role carries significant responsibility, and it is crucial that you understand the potential legal consequences that can arise from misconduct and negligence. These consequences not only affect your personal reputation but also undermine the integrity of the notarization process, potentially leading to legal actions and severe penalties. A notary public's duties are critical to the legal system, and when these duties are breached, whether intentionally or due to carelessness, the impact can be profound.

In California, a notary public is expected to perform their duties with diligence, accuracy, and impartiality. A notary must adhere strictly to the guidelines set forth by the California Secretary of State, as well as applicable laws and regulations. Failing to do so can result in a range of legal consequences, which may include civil liability, criminal penalties, or even the loss of your notary commission. Understanding these risks and taking steps to prevent misconduct or negligence is essential for any notary.

Misconduct by a notary can take many forms, but it generally involves intentional wrongdoing or unethical behavior. One of the most severe forms of misconduct is the act of knowingly certifying a false document. For example, if a notary knowingly certifies that a signer is present when they are not, or if a notary knowingly certifies that a document is accurate when it is not, this can lead to criminal charges. Under California law, this constitutes a felony offense, and the notary can be subject to both fines and imprisonment. A conviction for this type of offense is serious and can permanently tarnish a notary's professional reputation. In addition to criminal penalties, the notary may also face civil lawsuits for damages caused by their actions.

Another example of misconduct involves notarizing a document in which the notary has a personal interest or stake. For instance, if a notary is asked to notarize a document where they themselves are a party to the transaction, this could be viewed as a conflict of interest. Notaries are required to be impartial and to avoid any situation in which their neutrality might be questioned. If a notary fails to maintain this impartiality, they could face disciplinary actions from the Secretary of State, which could include suspension or revocation of their notary commission. This could also expose the notary to civil lawsuits, particularly if their actions lead to financial harm to one of the parties involved in the notarization.

Negligence, on the other hand, involves a failure to meet the expected standard of care that a notary should demonstrate when performing their duties. Negligence can occur when a notary makes errors due to carelessness or a lack of attention to detail, such as failing to properly identify a signer or not ensuring that all necessary information is included on the notarial certificate. While negligence may not always involve the intentional misconduct seen in more serious cases, it can still have severe consequences. A notary who is found to be negligent may face disciplinary actions from the Secretary of State, which could include a warning, suspension, or revocation of their notary commission.

One common example of negligence is failing to ensure that the signer is properly identified before completing a notarization. California law requires that notaries obtain satisfactory evidence of the signer's identity, typically through a government-issued photo ID or another reliable form of identification. If a notary fails to verify the signer's identity and subsequently notarizes a document without proper identification, this could lead to legal challenges and potential liability for the notary. In such cases, the notary could be held responsible for any damages caused by the improper notarization, including the possibility of civil lawsuits from the affected parties.

Another form of negligence is failing to properly complete the notarial certificate. The notarial certificate is a crucial component of the notarization process, as it provides a record of the notarization and ensures that the transaction is legally valid. If a notary fails to include all required information, such as the date, location, or type of notarization performed, it could cause confusion or invalidate the document. For example, if a notary fails to properly record the date on a document, the parties involved may later be unable to prove when the document was notarized. This could cause delays, disputes, or even financial losses. In some cases, the notary may be held responsible for any adverse consequences resulting from this oversight.

Another key area of potential negligence involves notarizing documents without ensuring that all signers are present at the time of the notarization. It is not uncommon for a notary to be asked to notarize a document for multiple signers, some of whom may not be physically present. California law clearly prohibits a notary from notarizing a document for a signer who is not in their presence. If a notary notarizes a document for someone who is not present or fails to verify that all signers are physically present, this could be considered negligence or misconduct. The notary could face disciplinary action from the Secretary of State, as well as potential legal liability for any issues that arise from the improper notarization.

The legal consequences of misconduct and negligence can be far-reaching. If a notary commits misconduct or is found to be negligent in their duties, they may be subject to civil and criminal penalties. Civil penalties could include the requirement to pay damages to individuals who were harmed by the improper notarization. In cases of severe negligence, the notary may be sued for financial losses that result from the invalidation of a document or the failure to properly notarize a transaction. This can result in substantial financial costs, including legal fees and compensation for any damages caused. In addition, a notary who is found guilty of negligence may face lawsuits from clients, businesses, or other parties who were affected by the notary's actions.

Criminal penalties for misconduct or negligence can be equally severe. If a notary is found to have intentionally committed fraud or other criminal acts, they could face felony charges, which carry significant penalties. These may include substantial fines, imprisonment, or both. Even if the notary's actions were not criminal, negligence can still result in misdemeanor charges, particularly if the notary's failure to perform their duties properly results in harm to others. For example, a notary who notarizes a document without verifying the signer's identity or fails to complete the notarial certificate correctly may be charged with a misdemeanor, resulting in fines and possible criminal prosecution.

In addition to criminal and civil penalties, a notary who engages in misconduct or negligence may also face disciplinary action from the Secretary of State's office. This may include suspension or revocation of their notary commission, which means that they would no longer be able to perform notarizations legally. The Secretary of State can also issue warnings or reprimands for minor offenses. However, even a minor violation can damage a notary's reputation and may make it difficult for them to regain trust with clients.

It is essential to understand that notaries are held to high ethical standards and are required to maintain accuracy, impartiality, and professionalism in all their notarial acts. Even small lapses in judgment can result in significant legal consequences. To avoid misconduct and negligence, notaries should take the time to familiarize themselves with the notary laws and regulations in California and follow them carefully. By doing so, notaries can help ensure that their work is above reproach and that they maintain the trust and confidence of the public. Proper training, attention to detail, and a commitment to professionalism are key to avoiding the legal pitfalls that can arise from misconduct and negligence.

# CHAPTER 8
## PREPARING FOR THE CALIFORNIA NOTARY PUBLIC EXAM

### OVERVIEW OF THE EXAM STRUCTURE AND CONTENT

The California Notary Public Exam is a critical step in the process of becoming a notary public in the state of California. This exam is designed to assess your knowledge of notary laws, ethics, and procedures, ensuring that you are equipped to handle the responsibilities and duties that come with the notary role. To help you succeed in this exam, it is essential to understand the structure and content of the test, how to prepare for it, and what to expect on exam day. This section provides an in-depth overview of the exam structure and content, offering clarity and guidance for aspiring notaries.

The California Notary Public Exam is a written test, consisting of 45 multiple-choice questions. These questions are designed to assess your understanding of the laws and regulations that govern notarial acts, your knowledge of ethical considerations, and your ability to apply proper notarial procedures in a variety of scenarios. The exam covers a wide range of topics that are critical to the notary's role in California, including document identification, legal procedures, responsibilities, and the legal consequences of misconduct. It is important to understand that the questions on the exam are designed to test your practical knowledge and ability to make sound decisions in real-life notary situations.

The exam is divided into several key areas, each representing a different aspect of notarial practice. These areas include:

1. **California Notary Law**: This section of the exam focuses on the legal framework surrounding notarial acts in California. It includes questions on the duties and responsibilities of a notary, the legal requirements for performing notarial acts, and the laws that govern the use of notaries in the state. You will need to have a clear understanding of the California Government Code, specifically the sections related to notarial acts, as well as other relevant state laws that apply to the notary profession. Questions may cover topics such as the proper identification of signers, the proper handling of documents, and the requirements for maintaining a notary journal.

2. **Notary Procedures and Practices**: This section tests your knowledge of the proper procedures for performing notarial acts. Questions in this area may include scenarios in which you need to determine the correct steps for taking an acknowledgment, administering an oath or affirmation, or certifying a copy of a document. You will also be asked about the proper procedures for dealing with issues such as signers who do not have proper identification, or situations in which a notary suspects that a document may be fraudulent. Understanding the correct procedure

for each type of notarization is essential for ensuring that your notarial acts are valid and legally binding.

3. **Ethical Responsibilities of a Notary**: This section evaluates your understanding of the ethical principles that govern notarial practice. It includes questions on topics such as avoiding conflicts of interest, maintaining impartiality, and handling situations where you may have a personal interest in a transaction. The California notary laws require notaries to act in an ethical and unbiased manner at all times. You will need to be familiar with the specific rules governing notary conduct, including the requirement to avoid notarizing documents in which you have a financial interest, and the importance of maintaining a neutral position when performing notarial acts.

4. **Recordkeeping and Journal Requirements**: A key responsibility of a notary is the maintenance of an accurate and complete notary journal. This section of the exam will test your knowledge of the requirements for keeping a notary journal, including what information must be recorded for each notarial act. You will need to know when and how to record the details of a notarization, as well as the requirements for maintaining the journal in a secure and accessible manner. The exam may ask you about the specific information you are required to record, such as the type of notarization, the name and address of the signer, and the type of identification presented.

5. **Fraud Prevention and Legal Consequences**: This section focuses on the potential legal consequences of misconduct or negligence by a notary, including criminal liability and civil penalties. Questions may include scenarios in which a notary is asked to notarize a document that appears suspicious, or where the notary suspects that fraud is being committed. You will be asked to demonstrate your ability to identify red flags for fraud, such as inconsistencies in the document, improper signatures, or issues with the identification of the signer. Additionally, this section will test your knowledge of the legal consequences for failing to follow notary laws and procedures, including potential fines, loss of commission, and even criminal prosecution.

The exam is designed to be challenging, but with thorough preparation, it is entirely possible to pass the test with ease. To prepare for the California Notary Public Exam, you will need to study the official California Notary Handbook, which outlines all of the laws, rules, and procedures that govern notarial practice in the state. The California Secretary of State's website is also a valuable resource, providing up-to-date information on notary laws, procedures, and exam requirements. Many aspiring notaries also choose to take an exam preparation course, which can help you familiarize yourself with the test format, practice answering sample questions, and reinforce your understanding of the material.

In addition to studying the California Notary Handbook, it is also helpful to take practice exams to assess your readiness. Practice exams allow you to get a sense of the types of questions that will appear on the actual exam and help you identify any areas where you may need to focus more attention. Time management is also important, as the exam is timed, and you will have a limited amount of time to complete all 45 questions. Practicing under timed conditions can help you become more comfortable with the exam format and ensure that you can complete the test within the allotted time.

On the day of the exam, it is important to arrive well-prepared and on time. You will need to bring a valid government-issued ID, such as a driver's license or passport, to verify your identity. You will also be required to take the exam in a secure, proctored environment. The exam is typically administered at Pearson VUE test centers throughout California, and you can find a test center near you by visiting the California Secretary of State's website. The exam is computer-based, and you will be able to review and submit your answers electronically.

After completing the exam, you will receive your results immediately. If you pass the exam, you will be issued a certificate of completion, which is a requirement for applying for your notary commission. If you do not pass the exam, you will have the opportunity to retake the test. However, it is important to note that there may be a waiting period before you can retake the exam, and you may be required to pay an additional fee.

While the California Notary Public Exam may seem daunting at first, it is designed to ensure that notaries have the knowledge and skills necessary to perform their duties competently and ethically. By understanding the structure and content of the exam, studying the relevant materials, and practicing with sample questions, you can significantly increase your chances of success. With the right preparation and focus, you can pass the exam with ease and move one step closer to becoming a licensed notary public in California.

## STUDY STRATEGIES AND TIME MANAGEMENT TIPS

Studying for the California Notary Public Exam requires dedication, focus, and a clear strategy. With the right study techniques and time management, you can prepare effectively for the exam and approach it with confidence. This section provides essential tips and strategies that will help you optimize your study sessions and manage your time efficiently to maximize your chances of passing the exam with ease.

One of the most important aspects of preparing for the California Notary Public Exam is understanding the structure and content of the test. It's crucial to know what you are being tested on and how to best prepare for the topics covered. The exam assesses your understanding of notary laws, ethics, procedures, and responsibilities in California. These areas include California notary law, notarial procedures, recordkeeping, ethical considerations, and fraud prevention. Each topic is essential for ensuring that you perform your duties correctly as a notary, and you'll need to demonstrate your knowledge in each area to pass the exam.

To succeed, it's vital to have a well-organized study plan that allows you to cover all necessary topics while giving yourself ample time to review and reinforce your knowledge. Effective study strategies will not only improve your understanding of the material but also enhance your ability to retain important information, ensuring that you are fully prepared when the exam day arrives.

First and foremost, *setting clear goals* is an important step. Knowing exactly what you want to achieve in each study session will help you stay focused and track your progress. You should break your study material down into manageable sections, prioritizing the most important topics based on your current understanding and the weight they carry on the exam. Set specific goals for each session, such as mastering a particular concept or completing a set number of practice questions. This method helps prevent the overwhelming feeling of having to study everything at once and allows you to focus on mastering one area at a time.

Another key strategy is *creating a study schedule*. The California Notary Public Exam requires a solid understanding of a wide range of topics, so it's essential to allocate enough time to study each one thoroughly. A good study schedule helps you stay on track and prevents last-minute cramming. Begin by setting aside dedicated time for study each day. This could be as little as 30 minutes or as much as several hours, depending on your schedule and how much time you have before the exam. It's important to be consistent—studying for short bursts each day is often more effective than long, sporadic sessions. Additionally, you should plan for regular breaks to keep your mind fresh and focused. A typical study session might last around 45 minutes, followed by a 10-15 minute break. This approach helps prevent mental fatigue and allows for better retention of information.

As you work through the material, it's essential to focus on *active learning* rather than passive reading. Simply reading the notary handbook or your study materials without engaging with the content may not be as effective in retaining the information. Active learning involves engaging with the material in a way that reinforces your understanding and retention. This can include summarizing what you've read in your own words, teaching someone else the concept, or writing down key points. *Making flashcards* is another powerful tool for active learning. Create flashcards for key terms, concepts, and legal terms related to notarial practice. Flashcards are an effective way to quiz yourself and reinforce your knowledge, especially for topics that require memorization, such as the various forms of notarial certificates or the specific legal requirements for notarizing documents.

One effective strategy for mastering the material is *practicing with sample exam questions*. The California Notary Public Exam is multiple-choice, so familiarizing yourself with the format of the questions is essential. Working through practice questions will help you understand how the exam is structured and the types of questions that are typically asked. You can find sample questions in study guides, online resources, or even in the California Notary Handbook itself. When practicing, focus not just on getting the answers correct, but also on understanding the reasoning behind the correct answers. Take time to review explanations for each answer, especially for the ones you get wrong, and use that feedback to improve your knowledge. It is also advisable to time yourself during practice tests to simulate the pressure of the real exam and get used to managing your time efficiently.

As you approach the exam, *reviewing key concepts* regularly is crucial. It's important to go over your notes and materials periodically to reinforce your understanding of the material and prevent forgetting key concepts. Before the exam, spend time reviewing your flashcards, notes, and any areas you feel less confident in. A final review session a day or two before the exam can be highly beneficial for cementing the most important information in your memory. However, it's important to avoid overwhelming yourself with new information in the days leading up to the exam. Instead, focus on consolidating what you already know and reviewing the topics you find most challenging.

In addition to studying effectively, managing your time during the preparation phase is crucial to ensure you can cover all material without feeling rushed or overwhelmed. *Time management* is a skill that not only helps with studying but also ensures you can effectively navigate the exam itself. The California Notary Public Exam has a time limit, and it's important to pace yourself while taking the test. In your preparation, practice pacing yourself by timing how long it takes you to complete practice questions or mini-tests. This helps you learn how to allocate your time wisely during the real exam.

Effective time management also includes knowing when to *stop studying* for the day. It's easy to fall into the trap of over-studying or trying to cram in extra material, but this can lead to burnout and reduced retention. By sticking to your study schedule and knowing when to take breaks, you can avoid the negative effects of fatigue and maximize your learning potential. Make sure you get plenty of sleep the night before the exam, as being well-rested is essential for mental clarity and focus on the test day.

Another helpful technique for managing time effectively is to *eliminate distractions* during study sessions. Find a quiet space where you can focus, free from interruptions or distractions such as phone notifications, television, or social media. Consider using tools such as website blockers to prevent distractions if you find yourself tempted to check social media or other non-study-related sites while studying. Creating a dedicated study environment signals to your brain that it's time to focus, which can improve the quality of your study time.

Maintaining motivation throughout your study journey is just as important as the study techniques you use. *Staying motivated* can be challenging, especially if you feel overwhelmed by the amount of material you need to cover. One way to stay motivated is by breaking your study tasks into smaller, more manageable goals. Celebrate your achievements as you reach each milestone, whether that's completing a chapter, mastering a particular concept, or finishing a practice exam. These small victories will help keep you on track and encourage a sense of progress.

Finally, it's essential to approach your study sessions with a mindset of *self-care*. Managing your stress levels and taking care of your well-being are key to successful exam preparation. Taking regular breaks, getting enough sleep, and staying hydrated are all important aspects of maintaining your focus and energy. Studying for an exam can be intense, but balancing your study efforts with self-care ensures that you can perform at your best.

By applying these study strategies and time management techniques, you will be better prepared to approach the California Notary Public Exam with confidence. With a clear plan, focused study sessions, and effective time management, you can set yourself up for success and pass the exam with ease. Stay dedicated, stay organized, and trust in your ability to succeed.

## SAMPLE MULTIPLE-CHOICE QUESTIONS WITH EXPLANATIONS

Here are several sample multiple-choice questions based on the topics covered in the California Notary Public Exam, along with explanations for each correct answer. These questions are designed to help you familiarize yourself with the types of questions you may encounter on the exam and to understand the reasoning behind each correct answer.

**Question 1:**
Which of the following is the *primary responsibility* of a notary public in California?

A) To act as a witness to the signing of documents
B) To verify the identity of the signer
C) To offer legal advice regarding the document being signed
D) To ensure that all parties are in agreement before signing the document

**Correct Answer:** B) To verify the identity of the signer

**Explanation:**
A notary's primary role is to verify the identity of the signer and ensure that they are signing the document voluntarily and without duress. This verification process may involve checking identification documents, ensuring the signer is aware of the contents of the document, and confirming that the signer is acting of their own free will. Notaries cannot offer legal advice, as this would constitute the unauthorized practice of law, and they cannot be responsible for ensuring that all parties are in agreement.

**Question 2:**
Which of the following documents *does not require notarization* under California law?

A) Deed of trust
B) Power of attorney
C) Lease agreement
D) Acknowledgment of a signature

**Correct Answer:** C) Lease agreement

**Explanation:**
Not all documents require notarization. For example, a lease agreement typically does not need to be notarized unless it is part of a legal transaction that involves recording or other legal procedures. On the other hand, a deed of trust, a power of attorney, and an acknowledgment of a signature often require notarization to be legally binding or recognized in California.

---

**Question 3:**
Which of the following *best describes the proper procedure* when a notary public is required to notarize a document where the signer does not speak English?

A) The notary must ensure that the signer reads the document before proceeding with notarization.
B) The notary can proceed with the notarization as long as the signer understands the document in another language.
C) The notary must rely on a translator to explain the document's contents to the signer.
D) The notary should refuse to notarize the document if the signer does not speak English.

**Correct Answer:** C) The notary must rely on a translator to explain the document's contents to the signer.

**Explanation:**
In California, when a signer does not understand English, the notary is required to rely on a neutral third-party translator to explain the contents of the document to the signer. The translator must not have any interest in the document and must act as a neutral intermediary to ensure that the signer fully understands what they are signing. The notary cannot proceed without ensuring that the signer is fully informed, which may require the help of a translator.

---

**Question 4:**
A notary public can refuse to perform a notarial act if:

A) The signer cannot provide identification.
B) The signer is under 18 years old.
C) The notary is not familiar with the document.
D) The signer is a relative of the notary.

**Correct Answer:** A) The signer cannot provide identification.

**Explanation:**
One of the essential responsibilities of a notary is to verify the identity of the signer. If the signer cannot provide acceptable identification, the notary must refuse to notarize the document. In California, acceptable forms of identification typically include a state-issued ID card or driver's license, passport, or a similar government-issued document. Age and familiarity with the document do not affect the notary's ability to perform the notarization, and a notary can still refuse

California Notary Handbook 2025

if the signer is a relative, as notarizing a document for a family member may create conflicts of interest.

## Question 5:
Which of the following must a notary public record in their notary journal when performing a notarial act?

A) The signer's social security number
B) The signature of the notary
C) The type of document being notarized
D) The notarization fee paid by the signer

**Correct Answer:** C) The type of document being notarized

### Explanation:
California law requires notaries to maintain a detailed journal of all notarial acts performed. The journal must include the *type of document being notarized*, along with other details such as the date of notarization, the names and addresses of the signers, and the type of identification presented. The notary's signature, social security number, and the notarization fee paid by the signer are not required to be recorded in the journal.

## Question 6:
Which of the following is the *most appropriate* course of action for a notary if a signer appears to be under duress while signing a document?

A) Proceed with the notarization as long as the signer provides identification.
B) Refuse to notarize the document and advise the signer to seek legal assistance.
C) Have the signer take an oath to ensure their signature is voluntary.
D) Allow the signer to sign the document in private to resolve any issues.

**Correct Answer:** B) Refuse to notarize the document and advise the signer to seek legal assistance.

### Explanation:
If a notary suspects that a signer is under duress or being coerced into signing a document, they must refuse to notarize it. A notary is required to ensure that the signer is acting willingly and not under any form of pressure or compulsion. If duress is suspected, the notary should advise the signer to seek legal counsel and cannot proceed with the notarization.

## Question 7:
A notary public in California must always ensure that:

A) The signer is over 21 years old.
B) The signer signs the document in the notary's presence.
C) The document is a legally binding contract.
D) The document is recorded with the county clerk.

**Correct Answer:** B) The signer signs the document in the notary's presence.

**Explanation:**
One of the fundamental requirements for notarization in California is that the notary must witness the signer's signature in person. The notary cannot notarize a document unless the signer is present and physically signs the document in front of the notary. It is not necessary for the signer to be over 21 years old or for the document to be a legally binding contract. The recording of a document with the county clerk is also outside the notary's responsibilities.

---

### Question 8:
Which of the following is considered *misconduct* for a notary public in California?

A) Charging a fee for a notarization that exceeds the maximum allowed by law
B) Refusing to notarize a document based on personal beliefs
C) Notarizing a document in which the signer is a relative
D) Performing a notarization without verifying the signer's identity

**Correct Answer:** A) Charging a fee for a notarization that exceeds the maximum allowed by law

**Explanation:**
Notaries are required to follow the fee schedule set by the state of California. Charging a fee that exceeds the maximum allowed is considered misconduct. While refusing to notarize a document based on personal beliefs may be ethically questionable, it is not necessarily illegal unless it violates California law. Notarizing a document for a relative is allowed, although it is advised against due to potential conflicts of interest. Failing to verify the signer's identity, however, is a clear violation of the notary's duties and can lead to legal consequences.

---

These questions provide an opportunity to reinforce key knowledge and principles required to pass the California Notary Public Exam. By practicing with these types of questions and understanding the explanations behind each answer, you can strengthen your grasp on notary laws and procedures in California. This approach will help you feel confident and prepared for the exam, ensuring that you are well-equipped to become a successful notary public.

California Notary Handbook 2025

## PRACTICE EXAMS TO ASSESS READINESS

This comprehensive practice exam consists of 50 multiple-choice questions designed to assess your readiness for the California Notary Public Exam. Each question has four answer choices, with the correct answer indicated. Detailed explanations are provided for each correct answer to enhance your understanding.

**1. What is the primary responsibility of a Notary Public in California?**

A) To draft legal documents
B) To witness the signing of documents
C) To provide legal advice
D) To administer oaths to witnesses in court

**2. Which of the following is NOT a valid form of identification for a Notary Public in California to accept when performing a notarial act?**

A) U.S. Passport
B) California Driver's License
C) Library Card
D) State-issued Identification Card

**3. A Notary Public must keep a journal of all notarial acts. Which of the following must be recorded in the journal?**

A) The type of document notarized
B) The signature of the signer
C) The notary's fee for the service
D) Both A and B

**4. What is the maximum fee a Notary Public in California can charge for taking an acknowledgment?**

A) $10
B) $15
C) $20
D) $25

**5. What should a Notary Public do if a signer does not understand the document they are about to sign?**

A) Explain the document to the signer
B) Refuse to notarize the document
C) Witness the signature and proceed with the notarization
D) Offer legal advice to help the signer understand

California Notary Handbook 2025

**6. Which of the following is a valid notarial act that a Notary Public in California is authorized to perform?**

A) Certifying a copy of a birth certificate
B) Administering an oath or affirmation
C) Providing legal advice on how to complete a form
D) Drafting a will

**7. A Notary Public must refuse to perform a notarial act if:**

A) The signer is not familiar to the Notary
B) The signer appears to be under duress or intimidation
C) The document is incomplete
D) All of the above

**8. What is the required identification for a person who is signing a document in California, if the signer does not have a driver's license or passport?**

A) A credit card
B) A government-issued identification card
C) A social security card
D) A voter registration card

**9. Which of the following is NOT a duty of a Notary Public in California?**

A) Verifying the authenticity of signatures
B) Certifying documents as true copies
C) Providing legal advice
D) Administering oaths

**10. What is the maximum penalty for a Notary Public who performs a notarial act without proper identification of the signer?**

A) Suspension of notary license
B) A fine of $500
C) Imprisonment
D) A civil penalty of $1000

**11. When performing a notarization, a Notary Public must be sure that the signer is:**

A) Able to read and write
B) A U.S. citizen
C) Not mentally impaired or under the influence of drugs or alcohol
D) An employee of the notary's company

# California Notary Handbook 2025

**12. If a Notary Public makes a mistake while notarizing a document, what should they do?**

A) Cross out the error and initial it
B) Draw a line through the error and write the correct information
C) Cancel the notarization and refuse to notarize the document
D) Void the document and restart the process

**13. Which of the following is considered an ethical violation for a Notary Public in California?**

A) Charging a fee for notarization
B) Notarizing a document without the signer present
C) Maintaining a journal of notarizations
D) Refusing to notarize a document because the signer is not familiar

**14. How long must a Notary Public in California retain their journal of notarial acts?**

A) 2 years
B) 4 years
C) 6 years
D) 10 years

**15. What is the penalty for a Notary Public who notarizes a document with false information?**

A) Civil and criminal penalties
B) Suspension of their notary license
C) A fine of up to $5000
D) Imprisonment for up to 6 months

**16. What does the term "acknowledgment" refer to in notarial practice?**

A) The process of verifying a signer's identity
B) The confirmation that a signer understands a document
C) The process by which the signer confirms that they are voluntarily signing a document
D) The signature of the Notary Public on the document

**17. A Notary Public is permitted to notarize a document for a family member in California under which circumstance?**

A) If the family member is a spouse
B) If the document pertains to a personal matter

C) If the Notary Public is neutral and does not benefit from the document
D) Never

---

**18. What must a Notary Public do if a signer refuses to provide identification?**

A) Proceed with the notarization based on personal knowledge of the signer
B) Refuse to perform the notarial act
C) Allow the signer to use a non-government-issued identification
D) Use an alternate form of identification not required by law

---

**19. A Notary Public can be held liable for which of the following actions?**

A) Incorrectly identifying a signer
B) Witnessing a document without verifying the identity of the signer
C) Charging more than the maximum allowable fee
D) All of the above

---

**20. A Notary Public is asked to notarize a document but the signer is unable to understand English. What should the Notary do?**

A) Proceed with the notarization, assuming the signer understands
B) Ask the signer to sign the document in front of a translator
C) Refuse to notarize the document if the signer cannot understand it
D) Translate the document for the signer

---

**21. What type of notarial act must be performed for a document that requires a signer to declare under oath that the contents of the document are true?**

A) Acknowledgment
B) Jurat
C) Oath of Office
D) Signature witness

---

**22. In California, a Notary Public is authorized to notarize a document that:**

A) Is being used for a court case
B) Has been partially filled out
C) Is signed by someone who is not physically present
D) Has missing or incorrect information

# California Notary Handbook 2025

**23. What must a Notary do before notarizing a document?**

A) Review the document for legal sufficiency
B) Ensure the signer is present and acknowledges the document
C) Provide legal advice to the signer
D) Verify the signer's relationship to the document

**24. Which of the following is true about a Notary's journal in California?**

A) The journal must include the Notary's personal information
B) The journal entries must be kept confidential and stored securely
C) The journal may be shared with anyone upon request
D) The journal may be kept electronically, but must be accessible only to the Notary

**25. If a Notary Public is asked to perform a notarization for a signer who is blind or visually impaired, what should the Notary do?**

A) Proceed with the notarization without any additional steps
B) Provide a written translation of the document in braille
C) Ensure the signer understands the contents of the document through other means, such as by reading it aloud
D) Refuse to notarize the document

**26. What is the required minimum age for a person to become a Notary Public in California?**

A) 18
B) 21
C) 25
D) 30

**27. If a Notary is performing an acknowledgment and the signer is unable to physically sign the document, what must the Notary do?**

A) Notarize the document without the signature
B) Allow the signer to make a mark in lieu of a signature
C) Refuse to notarize the document
D) Have the signer's representative sign on their behalf

**28. What should a Notary do if they suspect that a signer is being coerced or threatened to sign a document?**

A) Proceed with the notarization
B) Report the situation to law enforcement immediately

C) Refuse to notarize the document
D) Encourage the signer to proceed anyway

## 29. Which of the following is NOT a reason for a Notary Public to refuse to notarize a document?

A) The signer does not speak English
B) The signer is not the person they claim to be
C) The signer cannot provide proper identification
D) The document contains blanks

## 30. If a Notary Public receives a subpoena requesting journal records, what should they do?

A) Immediately provide the requested journal entries to the court
B) Notify the signer whose information is being subpoenaed
C) Contact the Secretary of State before releasing the journal
D) Refuse to provide any information under any circumstances

## 31. A Notary Public is asked to perform a notarial act for a person who appears intoxicated. What should the Notary do?

A) Proceed with the notarization as long as the signer has identification
B) Refuse to perform the notarial act
C) Notarize the document and leave a note about the signer's condition
D) Perform the notarization but ask the signer to sign again the following day

## 32. What must a Notary do if they are unable to verify the identity of a signer?

A) Notarize the document based on personal knowledge of the signer
B) Ask the signer to provide an alternative identification
C) Refuse to notarize the document
D) Provide a brief acknowledgment in writing about the difficulty verifying the identity

## 33. How long must a Notary Public keep their seal and other notarial records in California after their commission expires?

A) 1 year
B) 3 years
C) 5 years
D) 10 years

## 34. Which of the following acts is a Notary Public in California prohibited from performing?

A) Certifying a copy of a power of attorney
B) Drafting legal documents
C) Administering an oath for an affidavit
D) Taking an acknowledgment for a deed

## 35. If a Notary Public notarizes a document and later discovers that the signer did not understand the contents of the document, the Notary:

A) Can be penalized for misconduct
B) Is not responsible, as long as the document was signed willingly
C) Must redo the notarization with a new signer
D) Should inform the signer and refuse to notarize the document

## 36. In which scenario is a Notary Public in California allowed to notarize a document for a relative?

A) When the relative is the signer of the document
B) If the Notary is the party benefiting from the document
C) When the Notary remains impartial and has no financial interest in the document
D) A Notary can never notarize for a relative

## 37. What is required for a valid signature on a notarial document in California?

A) The signature must be legible
B) The signature must be witnessed by two people
C) The signature must be made in ink
D) The signature must be made in front of the Notary

## 38. If a Notary Public receives a request for a copy of their journal from a third party, what must the Notary do?

A) Provide the requested information as soon as possible
B) Contact the signer before providing the information
C) Refuse the request and ask for a subpoena
D) Inform the requester of the fee to release the journal

## 39. When performing an acknowledgment, which of the following does the Notary Public NOT need to verify?

A) The signer's identity
B) That the signer understands the contents of the document

C) The signer's willingness to sign the document
D) The legal validity of the document

**40. If a Notary Public's commission is suspended, they must:**

A) Continue performing notarizations until their suspension is lifted
B) Return their notary seal to the Secretary of State
C) Keep their journal and records for safekeeping
D) Request a new commission immediately

**41. If a Notary Public in California is unsure about the validity of a document being presented for notarization, what should they do?**

A) Notarize the document and let the signer handle any issues
B) Refuse to notarize the document and seek legal advice
C) Proceed with notarization, assuming the document is valid
D) Ask the signer to make changes to the document before notarizing

**42. What must a Notary do if they are aware that a document has been altered in any way?**

A) Proceed with notarization and include a note about the alteration
B) Refuse to notarize the document if it has been altered
C) Proceed with notarization as long as the signer affirms the document is accurate
D) Notarize the document and allow the signer to fix it later

**43. What should a Notary do if they notarize a document and later realize they made an error?**

A) Correct the error by adding a note to the document
B) Ignore the error, as it does not affect the notarization
C) Notify the signer and complete a new notarization with a correction
D) Destroy the document and refuse to issue a new notarization

**44. A Notary Public may refuse to notarize a document in which of the following situations?**

A) The signer appears to be confused about the document
B) The document contains a notarization clause
C) The signer claims they know the Notary personally
D) The signer refuses to provide identification

California Notary Handbook 2025

**45. What is the penalty for a Notary Public who intentionally notarizes a document that is false or fraudulent in California?**

A) A fine of up to $500
B) A warning from the Secretary of State
C) A possible prison sentence and revocation of the Notary's commission
D) Suspension of the Notary's commission for one year

**46. Which of the following is NOT a requirement for a valid notarial act in California?**

A) The signer must personally appear before the Notary
B) The Notary must verify the identity of the signer
C) The document must be legally binding in California
D) The signer must provide a thumbprint for every notarization

**47. What is the maximum fee a Notary Public can charge for a single acknowledgment in California?**

A) $5
B) $10
C) $15
D) $20

**48. If a Notary Public fails to maintain their journal or complete required entries, what consequences might they face?**

A) Suspension of their commission
B) Fines and legal penalties
C) Loss of notary status and a possible criminal record
D) All of the above

**49. A Notary is asked to perform an acknowledgment for a document written in a foreign language that they do not understand. What is the Notary required to do?**

A) Notarize the document and assume the signer understands it
B) Proceed with the notarization if the signer affirms understanding
C) Refuse to notarize the document and suggest a translator be present
D) Translate the document for the signer

**50. When must a Notary Public in California perform the notarial act?**

A) Before the document is signed by the signer
B) After the document is signed, but before it is filed with a government agency

# California Notary Handbook 2025

C) After the document is signed, while the signer is still present
D) Anytime after the document has been signed and witnessed

These 50 questions represent a well-rounded practice exam for those preparing for the California Notary Public Exam. By covering a wide range of topics, including legal responsibilities, ethical conduct, recordkeeping, and penalties for misconduct, candidates will be well-prepared to demonstrate their knowledge and readiness for the exam. Each answer and explanation has been provided to ensure that candidates can understand the reasoning behind each correct response.

## ANSWER KEY
Here is the complete answer key with explanations for all 50 questions:

### 1. What is the primary function of a Notary Public in California?
**Correct Answer: C)**
*Explanation:* The primary role of a Notary Public in California is to serve as an impartial witness to the signing of documents and to prevent fraud in legal matters.

### 2. Which of the following documents can a Notary Public in California notarize?
**Correct Answer: A)**
*Explanation:* A Notary Public can notarize documents such as wills, powers of attorney, and deeds. Notarizing a document ensures its authenticity.

### 3. In California, what is the minimum requirement for verifying the identity of a signer?
**Correct Answer: C)**
*Explanation:* The Notary must verify the identity of the signer by using valid, government-issued photo identification, such as a driver's license or passport.

### 4. Which of the following must a Notary Public in California record in their journal?
**Correct Answer: B)**
*Explanation:* A Notary must record each notarization in a journal, including the type of act performed, the document being notarized, and the identification provided by the signer.

### 5. A signer presents a document to a Notary but refuses to provide identification. What should the Notary do?
**Correct Answer: C)**

# California Notary Handbook 2025

*Explanation:* If a signer refuses to provide identification, the Notary should refuse to perform the notarization. Notaries must verify the identity of the signer before proceeding.

---

### 6. What is the penalty for a Notary Public in California who fails to maintain a notarial journal?
**Correct Answer: B)**
*Explanation:* A Notary who fails to maintain a journal may face administrative penalties, including fines or suspension of their notarial commission.

---

### 7. Which of the following documents does a Notary Public in California require the signer to personally appear for?
**Correct Answer: A)**
*Explanation:* A Notary must personally witness the signing of documents like deeds, powers of attorney, and affidavits. The signer must be present at the time of notarization.

---

### 8. What must a Notary Public do when they notarize a document that is incomplete or contains blank spaces?
**Correct Answer: C)**
*Explanation:* Notaries must refuse to notarize incomplete or blank documents unless the signer personally fills them in before the notarization.

---

### 9. If a Notary Public makes a mistake on a notarized document, what should they do?
**Correct Answer: B)**
*Explanation:* If a Notary makes a mistake, they must correct the error by properly acknowledging the mistake and, if necessary, completing a new notarization.

---

### 10. In California, what is the maximum fee a Notary can charge for an acknowledgment?
**Correct Answer: B)**
*Explanation:* In California, the maximum fee a Notary Public can charge for an acknowledgment is $15, as per state law.

---

### 11. When is a Notary required to refuse to perform a notarization?
**Correct Answer: C)**
*Explanation:* A Notary must refuse to notarize if the signer is not present, cannot provide proper identification, or is not willing to swear or affirm the truthfulness of the document.

California Notary Handbook 2025

**12. If a Notary Public is presented with a document that appears to be fraudulent, what should they do?**
**Correct Answer: C)**
*Explanation:* The Notary should refuse to notarize the document if they suspect it is fraudulent, as notarizing a fraudulent document could lead to legal and ethical violations.

---

**13. A Notary receives a request to notarize a document in a foreign language they do not understand. What should they do?**
**Correct Answer: B)**
*Explanation:* If a Notary does not understand the language of the document, they must ensure the signer understands it. If not, the Notary should request a translator to be present.

---

**14. Which of the following actions is prohibited for a Notary Public in California?**
**Correct Answer: D)**
*Explanation:* Notaries cannot provide legal advice or interpret documents for signers. They must remain neutral and impartial.

---

**15. What is the maximum fine that can be imposed on a Notary Public for misconduct in California?**
**Correct Answer: A)**
*Explanation:* A Notary who engages in misconduct could face fines of up to $750, as well as other disciplinary actions, including suspension or revocation of their commission.

---

**16. In California, how long must a Notary Public keep their notarial journal after the last entry?**
**Correct Answer: C)**
*Explanation:* A Notary must keep their journal for at least seven years after the last entry, which provides a record of all notarizations performed.

---

**17. Can a Notary Public in California notarize a document where they are personally involved?**
**Correct Answer: B)**
*Explanation:* No, a Notary cannot notarize a document in which they are personally involved or have a financial interest.

---

**18. A Notary in California is asked to notarize a document for someone who is ill and unable to sign. What should the Notary do?**
**Correct Answer: B)**

*Explanation:* A Notary should not notarize a document for someone who is unable to sign unless they have a power of attorney or another legal representative to sign on their behalf.

### 19. Which of the following is an acceptable form of identification for a Notary Public in California?
**Correct Answer: D)**
*Explanation:* A California driver's license, passport, or any other government-issued photo ID is an acceptable form of identification for notarization.

### 20. What should a Notary do if they suspect a signer is not acting of their own free will?
**Correct Answer: C)**
*Explanation:* If a Notary suspects that a signer is being coerced or is not acting of their own free will, they should refuse to perform the notarization and may report the incident if necessary.

### 21. A Notary is presented with a document containing a notarization clause. What should the Notary do?
**Correct Answer: B)**
*Explanation:* The Notary should verify the document's contents and ensure it meets all the requirements for notarization, but the Notary does not provide legal advice on the document's content.

### 22. When notarizing a signature, what must the Notary verify?
**Correct Answer: C)**
*Explanation:* The Notary must verify the identity of the signer and confirm they understand the document and are signing it willingly.

### 23. If a Notary in California is presented with a document from a person under the influence of alcohol or drugs, what should the Notary do?
**Correct Answer: B)**
*Explanation:* The Notary should refuse to perform the notarization if the signer appears to be under the influence, as they may not be able to sign the document knowingly or voluntarily.

### 24. If a Notary's journal is lost or stolen, what should they do?
**Correct Answer: A)**
*Explanation:* The Notary must notify the Secretary of State immediately if their journal is lost or stolen. They should also take steps to prevent further misuse, such as reporting the loss to local authorities.

California Notary Handbook 2025

**25. What is a Notary's primary responsibility when performing a jurat?**
**Correct Answer: D)**
*Explanation:* The primary responsibility of a Notary when performing a jurat is to ensure that the signer swears or affirms that the document's contents are true.

---

**26. What is required for a Notary to properly execute an acknowledgment?**
**Correct Answer: B)**
*Explanation:* For a valid acknowledgment, the Notary must ensure that the signer personally appears, is identified, and acknowledges signing the document voluntarily.

---

**27. A Notary is presented with a document containing a blank space for the date. What should the Notary do?**
**Correct Answer: B)**
*Explanation:* A Notary should ensure that the signer fills in all blanks, including the date, before the notarization takes place. The Notary must not notarize documents with blank spaces.

---

**28. Which of the following is a responsibility of a Notary Public regarding document integrity?**
**Correct Answer: C)**
*Explanation:* A Notary must ensure the document is complete and unaltered before notarization. Any incomplete or altered document must be rejected for notarization.

---

**29. What must a Notary do if they have a conflict of interest in the notarization?**
**Correct Answer: A)**
*Explanation:* If a Notary has a conflict of interest, such as being a party to the document or having a financial interest, they must refuse to notarize it.

---

**30. If a signer presents an expired identification, what should the Notary do?**
**Correct Answer: C)**
*Explanation:* A Notary must refuse to notarize a document if the signer's identification is expired, as the Notary cannot verify the signer's identity without a valid ID.

---

**31. How often must a Notary in California renew their commission?**
**Correct Answer: A)**
*Explanation:* A Notary in California must renew their commission every four years to continue practicing as a Notary Public.

California Notary Handbook 2025

**32. Which of the following would NOT be an appropriate method for verifying the identity of a signer?**
**Correct Answer: D)**
*Explanation:* A Notary cannot rely solely on personal knowledge to verify a signer's identity unless the signer has been personally known to the Notary for a long period (the law allows certain exceptions, but these are very limited).

**33. What should a Notary do if a signer refuses to swear or affirm that the document is true?**
**Correct Answer: B)**
*Explanation:* If a signer refuses to swear or affirm the truthfulness of a document, the Notary must refuse to notarize the document, as the notarization cannot proceed without an oath or affirmation.

**34. If a Notary receives a request for a notarization that violates California law, what should they do?**
**Correct Answer: A)**
*Explanation:* The Notary must refuse to notarize the document if the request violates California law or goes against the Notary's ethical obligations.

**35. What is the role of a Notary Public when it comes to a signer's signature on a document?**
**Correct Answer: D)**
*Explanation:* A Notary's role is to verify that the signer is signing voluntarily and that their signature matches the one presented for notarization. The Notary does not verify the content of the document.

**36. What is one of the most important ethical principles a Notary Public must uphold?**
**Correct Answer: C)**
*Explanation:* A Notary must always remain impartial and neutral, ensuring they do not have any personal interest or gain from the notarization.

**37. Can a Notary Public act as a witness to a document?**
**Correct Answer: A)**
*Explanation:* Yes, a Notary can act as a witness to a document, but only if they are not the same person as the person requiring the notarization.

**38. What type of document requires the Notary to obtain a thumbprint in California?**
**Correct Answer: B)**

*Explanation:* California law requires Notaries to obtain a thumbprint when notarizing documents related to real estate transactions, such as deeds and powers of attorney.

### 39. A Notary is asked to notarize a document in a foreign language. What should the Notary do?
**Correct Answer: C)**
*Explanation:* If the Notary does not understand the foreign language, they should ensure the signer understands the document's content, and if necessary, seek a qualified interpreter.

### 40. What action should a Notary take if a signer does not appear in person for a notarization?
**Correct Answer: A)**
*Explanation:* The Notary must refuse to notarize the document if the signer is not physically present, as personal appearance is a fundamental requirement for notarization.

### 41. If a Notary Public in California is unsure about the validity of a document being presented for notarization, what should they do?
**Correct Answer: B)**
*Explanation:* If a Notary is unsure, they should seek legal advice before proceeding with the notarization.

### 42. What must a Notary do if they are aware that a document has been altered in any way?
**Correct Answer: B)**
*Explanation:* A Notary should refuse to notarize an altered document, as alterations can compromise the document's legality.

### 43. What should a Notary do if they notarize a document and later realize they made an error?
**Correct Answer: C)**
*Explanation:* A Notary should notify the signer and complete a new notarization with the correct information.

### 44. A Notary Public may refuse to notarize a document in which of the following situations?
**Correct Answer: A)**
*Explanation:* A Notary must refuse to notarize a document if the signer appears confused about its contents or is not acting voluntarily.

## 45. What is the penalty for a Notary Public who intentionally notarizes a document that is false or fraudulent in California?
**Correct Answer: C)**
*Explanation:* Intentionally notarizing a false document can lead to legal and ethical penalties, including possible imprisonment and revocation of the Notary's commission.

---

## 46. Which of the following is NOT a requirement for a valid notarial act in California?
**Correct Answer: D)**
*Explanation:* A thumbprint is only required for certain types of documents, like deeds, and not for every notarization.

---

## 47. What is the maximum fee a Notary Public can charge for a single acknowledgment in California?
**Correct Answer: B)**
*Explanation:* The maximum fee for an acknowledgment is $10 in California.

---

## 48. If a Notary Public fails to maintain their journal or complete required entries, what consequences might they face?
**Correct Answer: D)**
*Explanation:* Failure to maintain a journal or complete entries properly can lead to suspension, fines, or criminal charges.

---

## 49. A Notary is asked to perform an acknowledgment for a document written in a foreign language that they do not understand. What is the Notary required to do?
**Correct Answer: C)**
*Explanation:* The Notary must ensure that the signer understands the document before notarization. If not, the Notary should suggest using a translator.

---

## 50. When must a Notary Public in California perform the notarial act?
**Correct Answer: C)**
*Explanation:* The Notary must perform the notarial act after the document has been signed, and the signer must be present during the act.

California Notary Handbook 2025

# CHAPTER 9
# POST-COMMISSIONING: STARTING YOUR NOTARY PRACTICE

## STEPS TO TAKE AFTER RECEIVING YOUR COMMISSION

Once you have successfully received your commission as a Notary Public in California, it is important to take the proper steps to ensure you are fully prepared and compliant with state laws and regulations. The process after receiving your commission is as critical as the steps that led you to this point. Following through on these steps is not only necessary to maintain the integrity of your practice, but also to uphold the trust placed in you by the public, the state, and the legal system.

The first step you must take upon receiving your commission is to *purchase your official notary seal*. This seal is essential because it is the symbol of your authority as a Notary Public. It must contain your name, the words "Notary Public," your commission number, the county in which your commission was filed, and the expiration date of your commission. It's important to note that only authorized vendors or suppliers may provide you with a seal. You cannot make your own seal or use an unauthorized one. Once you have your official notary seal, you should keep it in a secure location. As a Notary Public, you are responsible for ensuring the security of your seal, as misuse of the seal could lead to serious legal consequences.

The second step to take is to *obtain a notary journal*. A notary journal is required by California law to document each notarization you perform. This journal serves as a permanent record of your notarial acts and can be used in case there is a dispute or legal challenge regarding a notarized document. In California, the notary journal must include details such as the date and time of the notarization, a description of the document, the names and addresses of the signers, and the type of identification used to verify the signer's identity. The journal should also include a thumbprint for certain types of documents, such as deeds and powers of attorney. It's important to keep this journal secure and confidential, as it contains sensitive information.

Once you have your notary seal and journal, you should then take steps to *familiarize yourself with California's notary laws and regulations*. While you may have studied for the exam, it is essential to keep up-to-date with the latest rules, statutes, and regulations that govern notaries in California. You can do this by regularly reviewing the California Secretary of State's website, which offers resources and updates for notaries. Additionally, consider purchasing or downloading the California Notary Handbook, which is the official guide that covers all aspects of notarial law and practice. Becoming thoroughly familiar with the state's rules will help you avoid costly mistakes and allow you to conduct your duties with confidence.

One crucial step you should take after receiving your commission is to *notify your employer or any clients* that you are now a commissioned Notary Public.

This step is particularly important if you plan to provide notarization services as part of your job or business. You may want to update your professional resume, business cards, and any other marketing materials to reflect your new qualification. This can open up new opportunities for you in various sectors, from real estate to law, and even in financial services. Clients may seek out your services, knowing you can perform notarial acts.

Additionally, it is important to consider your *insurance and bond requirements*. As a California Notary Public, you are required to obtain a surety bond before starting your notarial duties. This bond protects the public in case of any mistakes or misconduct on your part. The bond amount is typically set at $15,000 for notaries in California. It's important to maintain this bond for the duration of your commission and to renew it if necessary. Some notaries may also choose to purchase Errors and Omissions (E&O) insurance, which offers additional protection against claims of mistakes or negligence. While not required by law, this insurance is highly recommended for those who frequently perform notarizations, as it can provide peace of mind and financial protection in case of legal action.

Another important step is to *understand the legal and ethical responsibilities* that come with your commission. As a Notary Public, you are entrusted with the authority to administer oaths and affirmations, take acknowledgments, and witness signatures. It is essential to understand that your role is one of impartiality and neutrality. You are required to act without bias and to ensure that the signer is competent, aware of the document they are signing, and doing so voluntarily. You cannot provide legal advice or offer opinions about the content of the document being notarized. Furthermore, if you are presented with a document that you suspect may involve fraud or coercion, you must refuse to notarize it. Your integrity is essential, and acting ethically is critical to maintaining your reputation and complying with state law.

Once you are up and running as a Notary Public, it's essential to *regularly review your notarial practices* and make any necessary adjustments. As you gain experience, you may encounter scenarios that require special attention, such as notarizing documents in foreign languages or notarizing for individuals with disabilities. The more you practice, the more confident and proficient you will become. However, it's essential to continually educate yourself on emerging issues and regulatory changes. Regularly attending workshops or seminars related to notarial practice can help you stay informed and connected with other professionals in the field.

In addition to staying educated, it's important to *ensure your physical and digital recordkeeping* is organized and secure. As mentioned earlier, keeping an accurate notary journal is required, but you should also maintain copies of documents related to your notarial acts, such as the signatures, identification copies, and any other information pertinent to the notarization. This will not only protect you in the event of a dispute but also help ensure you remain compliant with record-keeping laws. Furthermore, in today's digital world, many notaries are turning to electronic notarizations and digital recordkeeping. While electronic notarization is not yet widely adopted in California, you should be aware of any changes in this area. If you ever decide to transition to e-notarization in the future, be sure to check that you comply with all the legal requirements.

Once you are fully operational, you should also be mindful of *notary fees and billing practices*. While California law sets the maximum fees a notary can charge for certain services, it is important to be transparent with clients about your pricing. Charging excessive fees or failing to disclose your charges could lead to complaints or legal consequences. Make sure to keep your fee structure simple, clear, and compliant with state law. If you plan to provide mobile notary services, where you travel to the client's location to notarize documents, you can charge additional fees for travel time and expenses. However, these fees must also be reasonable and clearly stated upfront to avoid any misunderstandings with your clients.

It's also important to *know when to renew your commission* and how to keep track of the expiration date. As a Notary Public, your commission is valid for four years. You must submit your renewal application before your commission expires, or you will be unable to perform notarial acts until your new commission is issued. The renewal process typically involves completing an application, passing a background check, and taking the necessary oath of office. Staying organized and keeping track of your renewal dates will ensure there is no lapse in your ability to perform notarial services.

Throughout your career as a Notary Public, maintaining *good communication* with your clients is key. Whether you are working with individuals or businesses, being clear about your processes, the types of documents you can notarize, and any potential issues or limitations will help build trust and respect. Strong communication skills are vital when you are explaining notarial acts, answering questions, or addressing concerns. When you establish a reputation as a reliable, professional Notary, you will build lasting relationships and create opportunities for more work in the future.

By following these important steps after receiving your commission, you will not only ensure that you are complying with all legal and regulatory requirements but also set yourself up for success in your notarial career. The role of a Notary Public is both important and rewarding, and by executing your duties with care and attention to detail, you will become an indispensable part of your community and the legal process.

## BONDING AND INSURANCE REQUIREMENTS

In California, becoming a commissioned Notary Public requires more than simply passing the exam and receiving your commission. There are several legal and regulatory obligations that ensure the integrity of your notarial acts and safeguard both the public and yourself from potential risks. One of the most crucial aspects of your notarial responsibilities involves bonding and insurance requirements, both of which help protect the public and ensure that you conduct your duties professionally and ethically. Understanding the importance of these requirements, as well as the details behind them, is vital for anyone embarking on their career as a Notary Public in California.

When you are appointed as a Notary Public, California law mandates that you obtain a *surety bond* before you can begin performing notarial acts. A surety bond is essentially a form of insurance designed to protect the public from any financial loss that might occur as a result of improper or negligent actions by the Notary Public. It is a crucial element of your professional responsibility, offering a layer of protection for the parties involved in any notarized document. While the bond does not protect you as the Notary, it ensures that clients who are harmed by mistakes, negligence, or fraud on your part are compensated.

The *California surety bond* required for Notary Publics is set at a minimum of $15,000. This means that if you are found to have made a mistake, acted negligently, or engaged in fraudulent activities during the performance of your duties, the surety bond provides compensation to the affected parties, up to the bond limit. This bond also covers legal fees and court costs that may arise from defending against claims of misconduct. However, it's important to note that this bond is not a guarantee that you will be automatically protected in case of a dispute or mistake. The bond serves as a financial safeguard for the public, and it is your responsibility as the Notary to ensure that you act with the highest degree of professionalism and care to avoid triggering a claim against the bond.

To obtain the surety bond, you must go through an authorized insurance company or bonding agency that specializes in providing bonds for notaries. The process generally involves completing an application, which will require basic personal information, such as your name, address, and commission number. In addition, you may need to undergo a brief background check to ensure that you have no disqualifying criminal history. Once approved, you will receive a bond certificate, which you will need to file with the California Secretary of State's office as part of your commissioning process.

The bond itself is not intended to be a form of insurance for you personally; rather, it is meant to protect the public in the event that your actions cause harm. The bond does not cover situations where you make an honest mistake while notarizing a document. However, it may come into play if you are found to have acted with fraud, dishonesty, or gross negligence. It's important to understand that your bond may be called upon to settle claims or legal fees if someone alleges that you have caused harm through your notarial actions. Once a claim is made against your bond, you will be required to repay the bond issuer, and this could result in a loss of your bond and the inability to perform notarial duties until you secure a new bond. Depending on the nature and severity of the claim, you could also face penalties from the California Secretary of State's office or even legal action.

In addition to the bonding requirement, Notary Publics in California also have the option of securing *Errors and Omissions (E&O) insurance*, which is an additional form of protection that covers you for mistakes or omissions made while performing your notarial duties. While not required by law, E&O insurance is strongly recommended, particularly if you plan to provide notarial services on a regular basis or handle a high volume of notarizations. This type of insurance helps protect you against claims of negligence or errors that result in financial loss for your clients.

E&O insurance typically covers situations where you may have overlooked something, made an error in identifying a signer, or failed to follow the proper procedure for a notarial act. For example, if you accidentally fail to properly witness a signer's signature, and this leads to legal complications for the signer or another party, E&O insurance can provide coverage for the damages incurred. Unlike the surety bond, E&O insurance is designed to protect you personally, covering your legal fees and any resulting compensation you may be required to pay in the event of a claim.

The cost of Errors and Omissions insurance varies depending on the provider and the amount of coverage you select. While the state of California does not mandate that you carry E&O insurance, it is often considered a wise investment for any Notary Public who wants additional peace of mind. For instance, if you frequently perform notarizations for businesses or individuals in high-stakes industries, such as real estate or law, securing E&O insurance can help protect you from potential lawsuits. The coverage you choose can be adjusted to fit your needs, but it's essential to weigh the benefits of adequate coverage to safeguard against financial loss.

In addition to the basic bond and optional E&O insurance, some Notaries also choose to purchase additional *business insurance*, especially if they operate a mobile notary service. If you work as a mobile Notary, you travel to your clients' locations to perform notarizations, which can present additional risks, such as vehicle accidents or injuries while at a client's site. Business insurance can help mitigate these risks by providing coverage for liability, property damage, or injury claims. It is crucial to remember that while the state-mandated bond and E&O insurance cover specific aspects of your notarial duties, they do not provide protection for all the potential liabilities you may face in the course of running your notary business. By obtaining business insurance, you create a safety net to cover various other risks.

It's also important to be mindful of the *renewal process* for both your bond and any optional insurance policies you may carry. California Notaries Public are required to maintain an active surety bond throughout the duration of their commission, which lasts for four years. Before your commission expires, you will need to renew your bond by submitting a new bond certificate to the California Secretary of State. Be sure to stay on top of these renewal dates to avoid any lapse in coverage or ability to perform notarial acts. If you have E&O insurance, this policy will also need to be renewed before it expires. Keep track of the renewal deadlines for both the bond and insurance to ensure that you are always in compliance with California law.

Furthermore, it is essential to maintain *records* related to your bonding and insurance. Keep copies of your bond certificate, E&O insurance policy, and any related documents for your personal records. This documentation not only helps you stay organized but can also be valuable if you ever need to show proof of coverage during an audit or dispute. Maintaining these records is essential to keeping your business practices transparent and compliant with state regulations.

By understanding the bonding and insurance requirements in California, you ensure that you are legally protected, ethically responsible, and professionally secure in your role as a Notary Public. Whether you are just starting your notary career or have years of experience, staying informed and diligent about bonding and insurance ensures you can confidently perform your duties while safeguarding both your clients and yourself.

## SETTING FEES AND MANAGING YOUR NOTARY BUSINESS

As a Notary Public in California, setting fees and managing your notary business are critical components of your success and long-term sustainability. Whether you are operating your own notary business or working as a mobile notary, understanding the intricacies of fee setting, managing your time and resources, and ensuring that you are compliant with all applicable laws will help you navigate the responsibilities of your role effectively. Your notarial services are governed by state laws that dictate how much you can charge for various services, and the way you manage your business can directly impact your professional reputation, efficiency, and profitability.

To begin, it's important to understand that the state of California has established a *maximum fee structure* for the services you provide. This structure is clearly outlined in California Government Code Section 8211, which provides the official fee schedule for notarizations performed within the state. It's essential to note that the fees listed are maximum allowable charges, not minimums. This means that while you may charge up to the maximum fee set by the state, you are under no obligation to do so. You have the flexibility to set your fees within these limits, and this decision can be influenced by various factors, including your location, the complexity of the notarial act, and the type of clientele you serve.

For example, for a standard acknowledgment (one of the most common notarial acts), you may charge up to $15 per signature. However, if the signer requires multiple signatures or if you are performing the acknowledgment in an unusual or more complicated setting, such as in a remote location or at a time outside of normal business hours, you may find it reasonable to increase the fee. Similarly, for jurats, which are notarial acts that require the signer to swear or affirm the truthfulness of their statement, the fee may also be up to $15 per signature. Notaries may charge additional fees for travel if the notarization is performed outside of a usual office setting, which is often the case for mobile notaries.

It's important to note that while California law allows notaries to set their fees up to the maximum specified, the law also specifies that you must provide a *written fee schedule* upon request. This ensures transparency and allows your clients to understand exactly how much they will be charged for your services. The written fee schedule should outline the fees for various types of notarial acts, such as acknowledgments, jurats, and certified copies, as well as any additional charges for travel, after-hours appointments, or other special circumstances.

Providing a clear and concise breakdown of your fees can help build trust with your clients and avoid confusion or disputes regarding payment.

Beyond the fees set for individual notarial acts, there are also potential additional costs associated with running a notary business, particularly for mobile notaries. If you are offering notary services at a client's location or providing after-hours services, you may choose to charge for your travel time and expenses. For example, if you need to drive to a location a significant distance from your office or home, you may charge a travel fee based on the mileage or time involved. Keep in mind that while travel fees are not set by law, they must be reasonable and should be clearly communicated to the client upfront. It's also essential to keep records of these additional charges and make sure that your travel fee structure complies with your state's regulations regarding what constitutes a reasonable charge.

Aside from the cost of your services, another critical aspect of managing your notary business involves understanding *recordkeeping* requirements. California law requires notaries to maintain a *journal* of all notarial acts performed. The journal is a legal document and must be kept for a minimum of *seven years*. It is an essential tool not only for documenting the services you have provided but also as a safeguard in the event of a legal dispute. The journal must include specific details for each notarial act, including the type of notarization performed, the date and time of the act, the names and addresses of the signers, the type of identification provided, and the signature of the signer. These records help protect you from liability and ensure that you can prove you followed proper procedures if ever questioned about a notarial act.

As a Notary Public, your ability to manage your time and your clients' expectations will directly affect the success of your business. One way to improve time management is to optimize your scheduling system, especially if you are working as a mobile notary. You should always allow enough time between appointments to ensure that you can complete each notarization without feeling rushed. Plan your travel routes carefully to avoid delays, and communicate your availability clearly to your clients. With proper scheduling, you can avoid overbooking yourself and ensure that you can provide high-quality service to each client.

Another important aspect of managing your notary business is maintaining *professionalism* and *customer service*. Even though the fees you charge are set by law, how you interact with your clients can make a big difference in your reputation and in whether they choose to use your services again. Providing excellent customer service, being punctual, and maintaining a positive and professional attitude are all important factors in building client loyalty and word-of-mouth referrals. Remember that your notarial acts are a reflection of your integrity and professionalism, and clients who feel that they've received good service will be more likely to return to you in the future.

As you grow your notary business, you may also decide to expand your offerings. Many Notaries choose to specialize in specific areas such as *real estate notarizations*, *wills and estate planning documents*, or *loan document signings*.

Specializing in a particular area can allow you to charge higher fees, as clients often pay a premium for notaries who are experts in specific fields. Specialization can also provide you with a competitive advantage, as you will be able to cater to a particular set of clients who require specific services.

Running a notary business also involves ensuring that your business practices comply with all applicable legal and tax requirements. As a notary, you are considered a *self-employed professional*, and as such, you are responsible for your own taxes, including both income tax and, if applicable, sales tax on any goods or services you provide. You will need to keep accurate financial records of all the fees you collect, including any extra charges for travel, after-hours service, or special handling. It's also important to set aside a portion of your income for tax payments, as failing to do so can result in penalties. If you are unsure of how to manage your taxes, consider consulting with a tax professional who can help guide you through the process and ensure you remain compliant with state and federal regulations.

In managing your notary business, it's also essential to keep a close eye on your *professional reputation*. Your reputation as a notary is one of your most valuable assets, and how you manage your business practices will directly influence your success. This includes handling client interactions with respect, keeping accurate records, and ensuring that your notarial acts are performed with the utmost care and attention to detail. By maintaining a strong reputation for reliability and professionalism, you will be able to attract more clients and continue to grow your notary business over time.

Setting your fees and managing your notary business is not just about compliance with the law; it's about creating a successful, sustainable career that allows you to thrive while providing essential services to your community. With the right approach to fee setting, business management, and client service, you can build a successful notary practice that not only meets legal requirements but also positions you for long-term growth and success. By maintaining professionalism, staying organized, and continuing to expand your knowledge and skills, you can ensure that your notary business will be both profitable and respected in the marketplace.

## CONTINUING EDUCATION AND STAYING INFORMED

In the ever-evolving landscape of notarial law and practice, staying informed and up-to-date with changes to regulations, best practices, and new technologies is crucial to maintaining both legal compliance and professional excellence as a Notary Public in California. Continuing education is an integral part of your journey as a notary, not only to ensure that you pass the necessary exams but also to maintain your commission over time and provide the best possible service to your clients. Knowledge is the cornerstone of building a trusted, successful notary business, and ensuring that you stay informed about current laws and practices will enhance your ability to serve effectively and avoid costly mistakes.

The State of California places a high emphasis on continuing education for Notary Publics. Once you've completed your initial notary public training and passed the exam, there is still an ongoing need to expand your knowledge. California law requires notaries to complete a mandatory *Notary Public Education Course* as a part of their *renewal process*. These courses are designed to keep notaries current with any changes to notary law and procedures. While these requirements are specific to California, similar systems of required education are in place in many other states as well, and they emphasize the importance of keeping your skills and knowledge sharp.

Every four years, before you can renew your notary public commission, you are required to take a *6-hour education course* that covers various aspects of notarial duties, laws, and ethics. This course serves to reinforce your knowledge and understanding of California's notarial laws, ensuring that you continue to operate within the bounds of the law. Not only does this course help you stay compliant with state requirements, but it also helps you to continue growing as a notary. It's a proactive way to refresh your understanding of what you can and cannot do in your role, as well as learn about any legal changes that may affect how you perform your duties.

When it comes to *continuing education*, there are many opportunities beyond the mandatory course to enhance your expertise and build your notary business. Whether you are interested in a specific area of notarial practice, such as *loan signings*, *wills*, or *real estate transactions*, or if you prefer to broaden your knowledge about general notarial duties, many resources are available to help you further your education.

Local professional organizations and associations, such as the *California Association of Notaries (CAN)* and the *National Notary Association (NNA)*, offer ongoing educational programs, workshops, and webinars tailored to notaries. These organizations provide a wealth of information, covering everything from updates to California's notary laws to best practices for managing a notary business. By attending these workshops and becoming an active member of such organizations, you can ensure that you are always informed about the latest changes in the field. These educational offerings allow you to learn from experts in the notary industry, helping you develop the skills necessary to be successful in your notary practice.

Additionally, many companies that provide *notary supplies*, such as journals, stamps, and other tools, also offer training materials and workshops. These resources can be helpful in staying ahead of any procedural changes that may arise, particularly with regard to the tools you use to perform notarial acts. Staying informed about the latest products and technologies available can improve your overall efficiency, making your workflow more streamlined and easier to manage. Moreover, many of these resources provide guidance on specific niches within notarial practice, such as mobile notary services or the notarization of foreign-language documents. By exploring these specialized areas, you can further distinguish yourself from other notaries and offer a more diverse range of services to your clients.

In addition to formal education programs, another effective way to stay informed is through *self-directed learning*. This approach allows you to take ownership of your professional development by regularly reviewing resources such as the *California Notary Handbook*, which is the official guide provided by the Secretary of State. This handbook contains essential information on notary duties, responsibilities, and the laws governing notarial acts in California. The handbook is regularly updated to reflect any changes in the law and should be part of your ongoing study materials. Beyond the official state resources, reputable online platforms and educational websites often provide free or affordable resources, including blogs, videos, and articles that focus on specific aspects of notarial work.

For example, if you encounter a new notarial act, such as the notarization of digital signatures, it's important to stay informed about the legalities and technological tools involved. As remote online notarization (RON) becomes more widely available and accepted in California, learning how to handle digital notarizations and how they differ from traditional in-person notarizations will be essential. This type of technology-driven change is one of the most significant areas where continuing education plays a critical role. Staying ahead of the curve by learning about emerging technologies or the latest legal trends will ensure that you are prepared for changes in notarial practices that may impact your business.

Furthermore, as a Notary Public, you must be vigilant about any changes to state law that affect your practice. While continuing education courses help ensure you are up to date with the legal framework, you should also make a habit of checking for updates from reliable sources. The *California Secretary of State's website* regularly posts updates regarding notarial laws, including fee changes, new legal requirements, and any amendments to existing rules. In addition, the Secretary of State's office issues important *publications* and *bulletins* that can provide valuable information about your rights and responsibilities as a notary. Signing up for email notifications from the Secretary of State's website or subscribing to industry newsletters is an excellent way to stay informed and aware of any changes that could affect your business.

Another significant component of continuing education is *ethical practice*. Notaries are trusted individuals who handle critical legal documents that can have far-reaching consequences. Because of the seriousness of the role, notaries must be well-versed in ethical conduct and professional integrity. Continuing education programs often cover ethics training, and these courses are indispensable in ensuring that you adhere to the highest standards of professionalism and honesty. Ethical training includes understanding the importance of neutrality, recognizing potential conflicts of interest, ensuring that no coercion or undue influence is applied to signers, and properly identifying signers. As a notary, you must always conduct yourself with the utmost integrity and uphold the public trust.

Moreover, ongoing education helps you to *manage your business* more effectively. Whether you are working as an independent notary, a mobile notary, or as part of a larger organization, understanding how to navigate the administrative side of the business is just as important as your notarial skills. Many courses and resources are available that can teach you the basics of running a notary business, from managing your finances and setting your fees to marketing your services and ensuring that you maintain accurate records. A strong understanding of business operations will help you run a successful notary practice and keep your clients satisfied, resulting in repeat business and referrals.

In an industry where laws and regulations are constantly evolving, continuing education is a critical investment in both your career and your business. By actively seeking opportunities to learn, grow, and stay updated on legal and technological changes, you ensure that your notary practice remains compliant and competitive. Not only will this help you pass the required exams and maintain your commission, but it will also set you apart as a knowledgeable, trustworthy professional who can be counted on to handle any notarial needs. Whether you choose formal classes, self-directed study, or participation in professional networks, prioritizing continuing education ensures that you stay equipped to succeed in the ever-changing field of notarial services.

California Notary Handbook 2025

# CHAPTER 10
## RESOURCES AND APPENDICES

### GLOSSARY OF COMMON NOTARIAL TERMS

**A**

- *Acknowledgment*: A formal declaration made before a notary public by a person who has signed a document that the signature is their own, and that they signed it voluntarily.
- *Affidavit*: A written statement made under oath, used as evidence in legal proceedings.
- *Agency*: A relationship in which one person (the agent) acts on behalf of another person (the principal) in legal matters.
- *Authentication*: The process by which a document is verified as authentic, often by a notary or other authorized official.

**B**

- *Bond*: A financial guarantee that a notary public is protected against any financial losses caused by negligence or misconduct in their notarial duties.
- *Binder*: A record or collection of documents, typically kept by a notary or other professional, that serves as a reference or evidence.

**C**

- *Certificate of Acknowledgment*: A statement made by a notary confirming that a signer has appeared before them, verified their identity, and acknowledged the document voluntarily.
- *Certified Copy*: A true copy of a document made by a notary or other authorized official, with a statement confirming its authenticity.
- *Chattel*: Personal property that is movable, excluding real estate.

**D**

- *Deed*: A legal document that conveys the ownership of property from one party to another.
- *Document Authentication*: A notarial act confirming the authenticity of a document, often used for documents being sent abroad.
- *Duly Authorized*: A person or entity granted legal authority to perform certain actions, such as notarizing documents.

**E**

- *Electronic Notarization*: The act of notarizing documents electronically, where both the signer and notary can be in different locations.

- *Execution*: The formal signing or completion of a document, which may require witnessing or notarization.
- *Examination*: The process of reviewing a document to ensure that the signer is properly identified and understands the content.

**F**

- *Fraud*: A deliberate deception intended for personal gain, often a concern in the notarial field to prevent false signatures or misrepresentation.
- *Forgery*: The illegal act of falsely making or altering a document to deceive or defraud others.

**G**

- *Genuine*: A term used to describe something that is authentic or true, often referring to signatures, documents, or seals in notarial practices.

**H**

- *Hypothecation*: The act of pledging property as collateral for a loan without transferring ownership.

**I**

- *Identity Verification*: The process by which a notary confirms that a signer is who they claim to be, using reliable identification methods.
- *Impersonation*: When a person pretends to be someone else, a serious issue in notarial acts that must be prevented by proper identification.
- *Incapacity*: A legal term referring to a person's inability to make decisions or take actions due to mental or physical limitations.

**J**

- *Jurat*: A notarial act in which a person swears or affirms under oath that the contents of a document are true.

**K**

- *Know-Your-Customer (KYC)*: A process used by notaries and other professionals to verify the identity of their clients to prevent fraud and ensure compliance with laws.

**L**

- *Legal Capacity*: A person's ability to understand and make decisions regarding their own actions and legal affairs.
- *Lien*: A legal claim or right against a property, typically used as security for a debt or obligation.

**M**

- *Mandate*: A formal instruction given by one party to another, often involving authorization or power to act on their behalf.

- *Mobile Notary*: A notary who travels to various locations to perform notarizations for clients, often outside of traditional office settings.

## N

- *Notarial Certificate*: A document prepared by a notary that outlines the specifics of the notarial act performed, such as the date, type of act, and signatures involved.
- *Notarial Act*: A procedure in which a notary performs their official duties, such as witnessing signatures, administering oaths, or certifying documents.

## O

- *Oath*: A formal promise to tell the truth or perform a duty, typically sworn before a notary as part of the notarization process.
- *Official Seal*: A notary's personal seal or stamp, which is used to authenticate documents and provide evidence that the notarization has taken place.

## P

- *Power of Attorney*: A legal document that authorizes one person to act on behalf of another in legal or financial matters.
- *Protest*: A formal declaration made by a notary in cases where a negotiable instrument, like a promissory note, has been dishonored or rejected.
- *Public Official*: An individual who holds a position of authority within the government and is authorized to perform official duties, including notarization.

## Q

- *Quorum*: The minimum number of members required to conduct official business in a meeting or proceeding, which may include notarization.

## R

- *Recordkeeping*: The practice of maintaining accurate and organized records of notarial acts, often in a journal, as required by state law.
- *Revocation*: The official cancellation or termination of a notary's commission or a legal document's effect.

## S

- *Signature Witnessing*: The act of observing a person sign a document and confirming their identity, as performed by a notary.
- *Statutory Duty*: A legal responsibility defined by statute or law, such as the specific duties and responsibilities of a notary public.
- *Sworn Statement*: A statement made under oath, confirming the truth of the document's contents.

## T

- *Third-Party*: An individual or entity who is not directly involved in a transaction but may play a role in the notarial process.
- *Title*: A legal document or claim establishing ownership of property.

## U

- *Under Oath*: A phrase indicating that a person is sworn to tell the truth, often a requirement for making affidavits or taking depositions.

## V

- *Verification*: A statement or action confirming the accuracy of information in a document, often requiring a notary's certification.

## W

- *Warranties*: Legal assurances that the information in a document is true and accurate, often required for notarization.
- *Witnessing*: Observing the signing of a document to confirm that the signer is who they say they are and that they signed the document voluntarily.

## X

- *Xerox Copy*: A photocopy of a document; while not typically notarized, it may be involved in the document-handling process.

## Y

- *Yielding*: The process of producing or delivering something, which may refer to the proper execution of documents for notarization.

## Z

- *Zeroing in*: The process of focusing attention on a specific detail or aspect of a document during notarization, such as confirming the identity of a signer.

# CONTACT INFORMATION FOR CALIFORNIA NOTARY AUTHORITIES

**California Secretary of State – Notary Public Section**
- **Office Hours:** Monday through Friday, 8:00 a.m. to 5:00 p.m. (excluding state holidays)
- **Physical Address:** 1500 11th Street, 2nd Floor, Sacramento, CA 95814
- **Mailing Address:** Notary Public Section, P.O. Box 942877, Sacramento, CA 94277–0001
- **Phone Number:** (916) 653-3595
- **Email:** Notary Public (email form available on the website)
- **Website:** https://www.sos.ca.gov/notary

**CPS HR Consulting – Notary Public Examination Services**
- **Office Hours:** Monday through Friday, 8:00 a.m. to 5:00 p.m.
- **Physical Address:** 2450 Del Paso Road, Suite 160, Sacramento, CA 95834
- **Phone Number:** (916) 263-3520
- **Email:** notaryinfo@cpshr.us
- **Website:** https://www.cpshr.us/services-backup/california-notary-exam-2/notary-contact-information/

**County Clerk's Offices**
Below are contact details for several county clerk offices in California:
- **Ventura County Clerk-Recorder**
    - **Phone Number:** (805) 654-2263
    - **Website:** https://recorder.countyofventura.org/county-clerk/county-clerk/notary-public/
- **Sacramento County Clerk Recorder**
    - **Phone Number:** (916) 874-1645
    - **Website:** https://ccr.saccounty.net/Pages/Notary.aspx
- **Orange County Clerk Recorder**
    - **Phone Number:** (714) 834-2500
    - **Website:** https://ocrecorder.com/clerk-services/notary-public-registration

- **San Bernardino County Assessor's Office**
  - **Phone Number:** (909) 387-8307
  - **Website:** https://arc.sbcounty.gov/notary/
- **Kern County Clerk**
  - **Phone Number:** (661) 868-3588
  - **Website:** https://www.kerncountyclerk.com/en/notarypublic/

---

For comprehensive information on notary public services, including education, fees, and the official handbook, you can refer to the California Secretary of State's Notary Public page at https://www.sos.ca.gov/notary.

Made in the USA
Coppell, TX
25 February 2025